THE LAST OF THE
Fairhaven
Coasters

⚓

The Story of Captain Claude S. Tucker
& the Schooner *Coral*

ROBERT DEMANCHE, DONALD F. TUCKER
& CAROLINE B. TUCKER

Charleston · London

THE
History
PRESS

Published by The History Press
Charleston, SC 29403
www.historypress.net

Front cover: The *Coral* loaded with gasoline for Nantucket, 1920s. *Collection of Donald F. Tucker.*
Back cover, inset: Captain Claude S. Tucker at the helm of the *Coral*, mid-1920s. *Collection of Donald F. Tucker.* *Bottom*: The *Coral* at Taylor's Wharf, Fairhaven, circa 1950. *Courtesy of Captains Doug and Linda Lee.*

First published 2013

Manufactured in the United States

ISBN 978.1.60949.945.7

Library of Congress CIP data applied for.

*To the captains and crews
of the coasting schooners of old.
Their hard work and dedication
help build our nation.*

Contents

Preface

For many years, Captain Claude S. Tucker would entertain his wife and children with stories of his schooner days aboard the *Coral*. His son Donald found these looks back into history captivating, and in later years, he began to think others might feel likewise. It became Donald's goal, then, to set his father's stories down in print. In that way, future generations might get a flavor of the coasting life. Readers would also come to know the story of how at least one coasting schooner and the family that owned her continued to operate until near the very end of the age of commercial sail.

Three people contributed to the writing of this book. Donald delivered the first of many talks on the subject to a Mystic Seaport audience in 1986. In 1994, Caroline (Carrie) Tucker helped her father-in-law assemble photographs, transform his raw lecture notes into narrative and shape the work into early book form. I came on board two years later to develop their topic into a self-published book. Encouraged by that book's success, we now have launched an expanded and thoroughly rewritten take on Captain Tucker and the *Coral*. As we like to say, we have "overhauled our original work from stem to stern."

The story we tell is part "as told to" and part historical research. We were fortunate to be able to draw valuable information and insights from recorded interviews of Captain Tucker and of three others who spent some of their early years aboard the *Coral*—sons Bill and Donald and Bill Talbot. Other first-person sources include Captain Byron Hallock's *Forty Years Windjammer* and George Gale's *Log of the "Coral."*

A hurricane is pivotal to the story of Captain Tucker and the *Coral*. The story of a different hurricane will help convey my wish for the readers of our book. In the late summer of 2011, some friends and I had tickets for a concert at a nearby music venue. The venue was of the "theater-in-the-round under a big circular outdoor tent" variety. Unlike the hurricane in Captain Tucker's story, people knew about the impending 2011 storm well in advance, and management cancelled the show beforehand.

I learned of the cancellation by an email in which the author cheerfully signed off with, "Don't forget to button down the hatches!" Maybe it was nautical naïveté or just a subconscious slip. Either way, I got a kick out of it. I hope that, whether or not you know that one should "batten down" the hatches, you will learn something interesting from our book and have an entertaining time doing so.

Robert Demanche
Fairhaven, Massachusetts
March 5, 2013

Acknowledgements

The authors are especially grateful to Kathryn Eident for her editorial suggestions during this project's early stages; to both Dave Mitchell and Ted Lorentzen for their insights and suggestions for the manuscript; and to Dave Mitchell for his scanning and photography work.

The Tuckers lost almost all photographs, papers and other memorabilia relating to the *Coral* during the hurricane of 1954. We are deeply indebted to the following people and organizations that helped us reconstruct the story of Captain Tucker and the *Coral*: Captain "Biff" Bowker for his interview of Captain Tucker, and Bill Tucker and Bill Talbot for providing interviews; Bill Talbot; Charlie Sayle; Paul C. Morris; George Keyes; Captains Doug and Linda Lee; Ray Covill; Steve Crowley; Helen Tucker Davidson; Edna K.S. Demanche; Philip Arthur Hartley III; Barbara C. Whalen; John Wojcik; Joe Alcobia and the U.S. Coast Guard Auxiliary; the Fairhaven Office of Tourism; the Freetown Historical Society; and the State Library of Massachusetts for providing photographs and images.

We are grateful to Robert Sisler, historian for the Port Jefferson Historical Society, for directing us to Jeffrey T. Hallock, who brought *Forty Years Windjammer* to book form; Kathleen Brunelle and Stephen Cole for their suggestions on publishing; Captains Robert Douglas, Doug and Linda Lee and Ray Williamson for their interest and encouragement; and Deborah Chormicle for assistance with the bibliography. Thank you, also, to Professor Len Travers and Margaret Lowe for their timely suggestions.

We also wish to thank the archivists and librarians at the following institutions for doing the work necessary to maintain and make available the information that researchers find so valuable: the Millicent Library, the New Bedford Whaling Museum, the New Bedford Free Public Library/Special Collections and Archival Collections, the Thomas Crane Public Library, Cape Cod Community College and the U.S. Army Corps of Engineers.

And finally, thank you to all our family and friends.

CHAPTER 1

The Hurricane

Not long after waking, Bill Tucker climbed up the short ladder leading from the cabin and stepped out onto the deck of his father's schooner. He thought to himself, "This is starting out to be a beautiful day." In a few hours, Bill's father, Captain Tucker, would join him in Newport Harbor, and the two mariners would head to the island of Nantucket aboard their schooner loaded with two hundred barrels of paving oil. It was September 21, 1938, and the Great Depression was beginning its tenth year. Although there weren't many cars on Nantucket, this paving oil would help turn some old, unimproved road on the island into a street with a solid surface.

Their vessel was named the *Coral*. She could carry fifty tons of cargo, not a very large amount for a coasting schooner. Then again, out of all the coasters that ever sailed, she was one of a very few that still existed and could bring in at least a modest income. With 125 of the fifty-five-gallon metal barrels arranged to fill every possible space on deck and another 75 stored below, the *Coral* moved through the water so smartly that her captain could rightly claim, "She was a corker under sail."

A shipbuilder named Captain Henry Hallock built the *Coral* in 1878 in Port Jefferson on Long Island's northern shore. He built her as a sloop, a vessel with one mast, so that he could carry cargo on the sound. Within six months, though, he felt he would benefit by converting the *Coral* into a two-masted coasting schooner, a somewhat similar type of vessel.

The rebuilt *Coral* was family owned, like many other two-masted coasters. These wooden sailing vessels were relatively easy to handle and maneuver.

They were wide, for holding lots of cargo on deck, yet they could easily travel up into the numerous shallow inlets along the coast. They earned their keep by transporting various types of bulk freight. If they hauled lumber on one trip, they might haul oysters, vegetables, cordwood, brick or any of a number of goods and amenities on the next.

The carrying of cargo by a schooner dates back to before the American Revolution. But as time passed, new modes of transporting goods developed. By the end of the 1930s, the heyday of the coasting schooner was long gone. Charters to carry freight remained available but far fewer in number. For the Tuckers, the *Coral* brought in supplemental but essential income, about one out of every five dollars brought home. Besides that, Captain Tucker loved the *Coral*, and he had no intention of taking her out of operation as long as there was cargo to be delivered.

The state of long-distance emergency communications was primitive on the morning Bill Tucker stepped out onto the deck of the *Coral*. Before the day was through, the hurricane of 1938 would take most people by surprise and cause much devastation. It would be one of the worst New England storms since the days of the Pilgrims, and it would reach Newport Harbor before Bill's father did. Twenty-year-old Bill would have to face the hurricane in all its rage aboard an aging wooden sailing vessel. He would have to save the family's schooner from destruction, alone.

THE "GLASS" IS ANOTHER NAME FOR A BAROMETER, an instrument that measures atmospheric pressure. Bill Tucker saw that something was amiss at about ten o'clock that morning, when the level of mercury in the glass aboard the *Coral* started dropping...and dropping...and dropping. He took it as a sure sign he'd be seeing bad weather before long. By one o'clock he was even more certain. "And then the glass started skyrocketing down," was how he later put it.

A number of boats came into Newport Harbor and tried to anchor near the *Coral*, but they all left. Even a navy vessel came and went. None of their anchors would hold. The barometer continued heading downward, and although the *Coral* was at anchor, the wind kept thrusting the schooner backward.

Bill decided to try a standard procedure to keep the boat in place—running the engine at clutch speed. The reasoning was simple. Running the engine at clutch speed would push the *Coral* forward and help counteract the wind, making it easier for the anchor to hold. Bill went back and started the engine. Then he decided to run forward and set out a second anchor.

Now two anchors, one on each side of the bow, were in the fight to hold the schooner stationary.

The *Coral*'s yawl boat was a weighty version of a rowboat, and it had been floating behind the stern of the *Coral*, tied with a line. Bill knew he had to hoist up the yawl boat, for if it got filled with water, it would add that much more weight and strain on the anchors. He raced back to the stern again and pulled on the line of the block and tackle to try to raise and secure the yawl boat, but the weight was too much for him. He could only lift it just clear of the water.

Up forward, the windlass was bolted solid to the deck, just ahead of the foremast. When the anchors were raised, their chains would wrap around the windlass. Bill saw that the wind was starting to pull the windlass right off the deck. If the windlass were to separate from the deck, it would go crashing through the bow, and the *Coral* would be set adrift, at the mercy of the storm. So, Bill ran up forward again to try to prevent the windlass from breaking free by wrapping a utility chain around the foremast and using it to shackle both anchor chains together.

Bill then heard the sound of one of the anchor chains parting (breaking in two). This left the *Coral* holding on with only one anchor. But as the engine kept moving the *Coral* forward, the schooner pivoted on the remaining anchor and swung sideways. As she did, the yawl boat that hung just above the waves dipped down below the surface. The weight of the water rushing in pulled the yawl boat even farther downward, and the line and block and tackle followed it into the drink. Bill heard the engine start to labor and hurried aft, but it was too late. The line had snarled the propeller, and the engine seized up.

With the engine dead and only one anchor holding, the *Coral* could do nothing but drift. She finally hit Goat Island between the ferry slip and the navy torpedo station, "just as if you steered it through," as Bill would later recall. The waves continued to pound the *Coral*'s starboard (right) side against the rocks until the storm eventually lost its punch.

Before long, Bill made it safely off the *Coral* and onto the shore at Goat Island. A few days later, the schooner was refloated and towed back to Fairhaven. Captain Tucker had the *Coral* hauled out on the marine railway at Peirce and Kilburn's, now Fairhaven Shipyard South. The repair work began, but the money to do the work eventually ran out. The workmen only got as far as replacing many of the ribs and re-planking the hull. This small, veteran coaster would never carry another cargo.

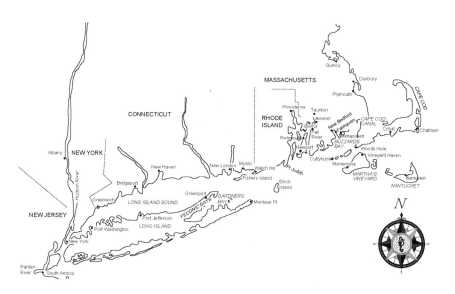

Chart of the coastal areas of southern New England and Long Island. *Illustration by Michael Smith; Collection of Donald F. Tucker.*

The damage inflicted by the hurricane was extensive, as seen in this photograph of the *Coral* hauled out at Peirce and Kilburn shipyard, Fairhaven. *Photograph by Albert Cook Church; Collection of Donald F. Tucker.*

LOOKING BACK TODAY, the thought of the *Coral*'s demise might bring forth a feeling of sadness, or at least wistfulness, that we will never again see the sight of her masts reaching above the rooftops along Fairhaven's waterfront. On the other hand, it is a wonder that Captain Tucker and the *Coral* continued to haul cargoes for as long as they did into the twilight years of the age of commercial sail.

How could the *Coral* have lasted so long? Who was this Captain Tucker who owned and sailed the *Coral* for the last third of her sixty-year career, and why did it matter that Fairhaven was their home? Why was this type of vessel and the work it did so important in the first place?

CHAPTER 2

"The Most Visible Species of Vessel"

From the time our nation was still a collection of colonies until well into the 1800s, there were relatively few roads. The ones that existed were so primitive and inferior that the only effective way to carry large amounts of cargo was by coastal waterways and rivers. Sloops and schooners were often engaged in this trade among the colonies. The victory at Yorktown in 1781 sealed our struggle for independence, and by the time trade resumed in the following years, the two-masted schooner had established itself as the preferred coastal cargo carrier.

A schooner is typically a wooden vessel with two or more masts. Its sails are oriented fore and aft, like a sailboat, whereas the square sails of a ship run from side to side. The schooner usually operates within easy reach of shore while the ship must withstand the rigors of the open ocean. There were several types of schooners, designed and built for various purposes. Some were built for fishing or whaling while others were made as pilot schooners or schooner yachts. Some were used as privateers while others transported Christmas trees, smuggled bootleg alcohol or carried human beings to be sold into slavery.

Coasting, or coastal, schooners were economical and practical to both build and operate. Mariners considered them to be weatherly, maneuverable and handy. Because the sails were fewer and their arrangement fore and aft made them easier to manage, far fewer crew members were required. The shallow draft (the depth of water required) meant that the vessel could go up into the numerous bays and coastal inlets easily. The beam (width), which is wide in coasters, provided ample room to carry cargo on deck and below.

Layout of buildings at Cook Borden and Company, Fall River. Note the numerous schooners and a few sloops nearby in the Taunton River. Pre-1883. *Courtesy of the State Library of Massachusetts.*

THE LATTER HALF OF THE 1800s was an era of industrialization, especially in the Northeast. The transportation of bulk cargo was vital. These cargoes were varied: coal to provide energy to power machinery; coal and wood for heat; lumber, brick, limestone and granite for constructing houses, public buildings and wharves; crops; farming implements and household goods; and bulk quantities of anything and everything else necessary for daily life. Thousand of coasting schooners worked along our coasts. The coasting schooner was the eighteen-wheeler of its day.

By midcentury, a system of railroads had developed and was especially extensive in New England. Still, the necessity for water transport required that many larger, three-masted schooners be built. The coaster became so numerous that historian W.H. Bunting declared in *Portrait of a Port: Boston, 1852–1914*, "The coasting schooner was simply the most visible species of vessel inhabiting the port of Boston during the latter half of the nineteenth century."

After the Civil War, the cities and towns of New England grew tremendously. Schooners sailed from port to port and carried many of the goods required to fuel this growth. As the country industrialized, many new mills appeared on the landscape, and great waves of immigrants came to work in them. These mills needed power to operate, and the multitudes of new workers needed housing, which did not yet exist.

The burgeoning population required lumber from Maine for new homes and factories. "One has only to look at the dwellings and tenements built during the last quarter of the nineteenth century and still to be seen in some of our cities," historian Charles S. Morgan wrote, "to realize that in late Victorian gingerbread and gimcrack architecture nobody used one piece of lumber where three or four could be made to do." Maine also sent ice for refrigeration, granite and lime to make building mortar and brownstone to construct buildings and public projects. Schooners freighted the sand that the foundries used to make molds for iron implements and the clay used for brick. Maine in turn imported southern oak and hard pine to build more and bigger schooners. Throughout the Northeast, coasters carried vegetables and fruits, seafood, farming implements and goods used in the home.

Coal, a source of energy, emerged onto the scene even before the Civil War. Coal mined in states to the south of New England made its way north in increasingly greater quantities, mostly transported by the large coasting schooners. Bituminous coal fueled the mills and railroad locomotives as well as the power plants that generated the electricity for homes and street railway cars. The growing populace burned anthracite coal to heat their homes and buildings.

It was during this period that Captain Henry Hallock of Port Jefferson, Long Island, built a cargo-carrying sloop and named her the *Coral*. She was a wooden sailing vessel that would continue to find work for the next sixty years.

CAPTAIN HALLOCK BUILDS THE *CORAL*

The village of Port Jefferson, on the north side of Long Island, was alive with maritime activity in late April 1878 when Byron Hallock turned fifteen years old. The village was the home of coastal schooner captains, blue water sailors and seamen, as well as a shipbuilding industry that was the largest in Suffolk County, New York. Byron's father was Captain Henry Hendrickson Hallock, a shipbuilder of note in the community.

Henry Hallock had just completed a stout little sloop named the *Coral*. His son Byron would become master of the *Coral* before he reached the age of eighteen. Later in life, Byron wrote extensively about his own maritime experiences, and his son, Albert G. Hallock, edited this narrative to produce the book *Forty Years Windjammer*.

Captain Hallock intended the *Coral* to be used in general freighting between New York and ports on Long Island Sound, "or elsewhere as chance might offer." But before the little sloop would carry her first cargo, the company that operated a menhaden fertilizer factory at the eastern end of Long Island proposed something different. It wanted to charter the *Coral* to tow two dories and a large net out to the fishing area and bring home the catch. With the menhaden fishing industry in its prime and boats like the *Coral* in demand, this looked more profitable than carrying cargo. Captain Hallock took the offer.

The *Coral* spent her first spring and summer in the menhaden fishery, with Byron Hallock as a member of the crew for the first two months. One day in September 1878 while back in Port Jefferson, Byron took a walk down to one of the docks and was very surprised to discover the *Coral* anchored in the harbor, abandoned by the fertilizer company and looking, as he wrote, "very unshipshape…the dirtiest-looking vessel I had ever been aboard, and she not yet a year old!"

Within two months, Captain Hallock undertook the extensive work of converting the *Coral* to a schooner rig, and he brought her back to respectability with a thorough cleaning, fumigating and painting. The transformed *Coral* was now re-rigged with two masts, each with a topsail. At the bow were a forestaysail, jib and jibtopsail. The boat was fifty-four feet, seven inches long,

The *Coral*. Date and location unknown. *Collection of Donald F. Tucker.*

nineteen feet, five inches abeam and drew six feet, four inches loaded and five feet, two inches light. A roomy, comfortable cabin was situated aft with a well-equipped galley up forward.

Captain Hallock now returned the *Coral* to her original purpose—freighting. During the next few years, the *Coral* transported Chesapeake Bay oysters to Baltimore during the winter (a lucrative endeavor) and carried various cargoes in the waters from Buzzards Bay to Chesapeake Bay during the summer. The freight included cordwood, gravel, fruits, vegetables and pig iron. At age seventeen, Hallock's son, Byron, became captain.

The *Coral* experienced many adventures during her early years, including surviving a terrifying night of treacherous weather off Virginia's coast. The inexperienced Captain Byron dealt successfully with these situations, however, and later wrote of one storm, "One very important factor in our favor was that we had under us as fine a seaboat as there was in our fleet of oystermen. We needed it that night!"

One night, a heavy fog lay off Point Judith. It was "dark as a pocket and thick as pudding," and a Fall River Line steamer stopped just in time to avoid plowing into the *Coral*. On another dark night off Falkner Island not far from New Haven, the *Coral* ran into a squall and had to haul down all sails. Before long, a passing steamer collided with her and left the *Coral* without a bowsprit.

Perhaps the most frightening event for Captain Byron occurred on his first trip as master of the *Coral*. Captain Byron Hallock took on two crew members for a charter that began in late December 1880 and extended into the following month. Aboard the *Coral* on the last leg of the trip was nearly $7,000 worth of oysters bound from the Piankatank River in Virginia to Baltimore. The vessel herself was worth another $6,000. Maybe it was the money or maybe they didn't like the captain, but in any event, the two crewmen mutinied.

It was a tense two days. Early in the ordeal, the young captain subdued one of the crewmen by applying a four-legged stool to his head, and he kept the other at bay by threatening to use his revolver. On the last day of the trip, before 7:00 a.m. had even arrived, another scuffle ensued, but again Captain Byron maintained control. Drawing his pistol, he ordered the two to stay down below in the fo'c'sle, the crew's quarters below deck at the bow of the vessel. (Fo'c'sle is a contraction of "forecastle," much easier to pronounce—fōk-sle—than it is to spell.) Captain Byron sailed solo for the remaining fourteen hours that it took to reach Baltimore, all the while keeping an eye out for his attackers. By the time the *Coral* finally reached port at ten o'clock that night, he had gone twenty-three hours with little to eat. Captain Byron took the yawl boat ashore to summon

A schooner in Maryland hauling cordwood. Note the yawl boat hanging from the davits on the stern. The helmsman's line of sight is just above the top of the stack of cordwood. *Photograph by George Keyes; Collection of Donald F. Tucker.*

the police, but while he was gone, the mutineers absconded. The ordeal may have been over but the "nerve strain of the whole thing" lingered, as the captain put it.

By March 1884, Captain Byron Hallock was nearly twenty-one years old and had spent five winters in the oyster trade in and around Chesapeake Bay and five summers in general freighting wherever a charter could be found. He decided to leave the *Coral* at this time and to ship aboard the *Vega*, a schooner yacht large enough to draw ten feet of water. After considering the pros and cons, he enthusiastically looked forward to working aboard his new place of employment:

> *I decided to try yachting as that seemed to be an occupation that was more promising, and offered better pay, especially if I could become master of a yacht.*
>
> *The* Vega's *accommodations both fore and aft were of the best. There was a large galley, and as Bert Gildersleeve could certainly "sling the hash," we crewmen lived high. No expense was spared to give us the best the market afforded.*

CHAPTER 3

New Owners, New Competition

Throughout the 1880s and '90s, the *Coral* changed hands several times. She was often enrolled at New London, occasionally at Greenport on Long island and Providence up north, and Crisfield, Maryland, and Norfolk, Virginia, in the Chesapeake Bay area.

The two- and three-masted schooners continued to find cargoes to carry during these decades. The growing need to transport huge amounts of coal for heating, cooking and producing electricity spurred the building of larger and larger capacity schooners, and the larger three-masters transported much of the nation's coal even until the end of the 1880s. The growth in the size of schooners was most visible, however, in the increased number of masts on the vessels. In the 1880s, many four-masted schooners were launched. The trend continued at the turn of the century with the building of many five- and six-masters and even one seven-master.

Another form of transporting goods, however, was the railroad, which continued to seize its share of the business. So, too, did the combination of a steam tugboat towing one or more barges. The tug-and-barge configuration became so successful that the years following the turn of the century signaled the beginning of the end for the schooner trade.

The steam tug-and-barge combination had distinct advantages over the solitary schooner. It could ignore the whims of the wind and go where it pleased whenever it pleased, which a schooner could not. The steam tug-and-barge could carry more coal per trip than could one schooner. Moreover, a tug could drop off its loaded barges at a destination and immediately pick up other loaded barges without having to wait to unload before heading for its next port. A schooner had to unload one load before taking on another.

The new method was not a perfect solution, however. Towing a barge is an inherently dangerous operation, especially when the tug would tow two strings of several barges each. The strings of barges could be difficult to control and would sometimes spread widely, creating a danger to other vessels.

Still, the steam tug-and-barge was a successful means of moving cargo. These barges were at first simply the hulls of schooners and ships that could no longer find work during the economic depression of the 1890s. Some schooner owners even converted their vessels to barges by cutting down the masts. In later years, barges were flat-decked carriers built specifically for that purpose. It would not be long before the motor truck, a new alternative, would make its presence felt.

Nevertheless, there were reasons why the railroad, tug-and-barge and truck did not carry certain cargoes to certain destinations. These niche markets remained available to the coasting schooner, and so some coasters, such as the *Coral*, continued to find work.

Sometime between 1905 and 1915, Irving D. Talbot became owner of the *Coral*. Before his career was over, Captain Talbot would own other coasters, including the *George F. Carman*, the *Jenny Z.* and the *Gallup*, as well as shares in the *B.F. Jayne* and the 250-ton *LaForest L. Simmons*.

The statistical tide may have officially begun to turn in favor of steam, but Captain Talbot continued to find a variety of cargoes that required hauling, cargoes such as brick, coal and oysters as well as cordwood from Assonet (a village in the town of Freetown).

Captain Irving D. Talbot. *Courtesy of Wilfred D. Talbot.*

Wilfred D. "Bill" Talbot, son of Captain Irving D. Talbot. October 11, 1996. *Courtesy of Robert Demanche.*

The captain's son sometimes accompanied his father aboard the *Coral* until 1915, the year Captain Talbot sold the schooner. Bill Talbot was ten years old at the time, and he went on to work aboard schooners until about 1929. He also worked as a purser on the SS *Nobska*, a steamer that ran from New Bedford to Martha's Vineyard and Nantucket. Bill's grandfather George E. Brown had been a whaling captain out of New Bedford, Fall River, and New London.

SELLERS, SCHOONER CAPTAINS AND BUYERS handled their business arrangements in several ways to assist in orderly payment and to see that a cargo reached its destination on time and in good condition. One type of arrangement was the "charter party." This was a contract in which a captain agreed to use his schooner to haul a particular cargo for the seller from one location to another. The charter party would specify how much time was allowed for loading and unloading as well as the agreed-on amount owed. The seller would own the cargo, carry any insurances on it and be otherwise responsible for the cargo until the buyer received it.

A second way was to make an agreement on a handshake. Captain Talbot usually did things this way for all types of cargo except one. As his son Bill explained in an interview, "Oysters you had to have a home for."

A third method was for the captain to simply buy the cargo and trust that the buyer would pay when the cargo was delivered. In this case, the captain took all the risk, but a track record of honesty and reliability on the buyer's part usually meant the risk was minimal. This is the arrangement that Captain Talbot had with a customer on Martha's Vineyard. Bill Talbot later recalled a story about how this trust was not misplaced.

On one occasion, Captain Talbot and Bill delivered fifty tons of coal to the little fishing village of Menemsha on Martha's Vineyard. As the *Coral* approached the dock, a Mr. Reed came out of the store he ran there. He brought out a ram's horn, and as he blew it, a group of Wampanoag Indians appeared. The unloading began, and the Wampanoags put the coal in piles. Perhaps it had been a long day because at that point, Captain Talbot said, "Come on, Bill. Let's go down the fo'c'sle and have dinner. I can't keep track of this."

With the unloading and the business taken care of, the *Coral* headed home. While they were heading up the Sakonnet River, to the east of Middletown and Portsmouth, Rhode Island, Captain Talbot said, "Bill, we didn't do bad. I had fifty ton on and I got slips for forty-eight."

The following January, Captain Talbot received a letter from Mr. Flanders, the superintendent of schools in Chilmark on the Vineyard. He had written, "Captain, I'm very sorry. I owe you for two tons of coal. Here's the check. We had to. We'd run out of money."

Bill Talbot concluded his story, "Honest people down there."

Bill remembered another occasion when the buyer's "assets" had frozen. It was cold out the night Captain Talbot received the telephone call. The caller sounded hurried. Not only did he sound hurried, but he also *was* hurried. He was building a powder (ammunition) house on Rose Island off Newport and facing a deadline, but he was somehow short of bricks and needed help fast. The captain was hesitant to take on this job, but he and Bill, nevertheless, set out in the *Coral* for the Stiles & Hart brickyard in the far upper reaches of the Taunton River.

At the brickyard, the loading began. In an attempt to save time and get the vessel moving again, the workers loading the *Coral* were told to stray from the usual procedure. As Bill Talbot later explained, "We put no boards between 'em, no straw. Well, it froze over night, and we had a hell of a job getting them off of the boat. I forget if they had any steam or whatever to get 'em off."

As time went on, Captain Talbot continued to own and operate the *Coral*. That all changed one day in 1915 when the captain happened to see a familiar face at the dock in Fall River and called out, "Tucker, you want to buy a boat?"

CHAPTER 4

From Farm Boy to Mariner

The young man whom Captain Talbot called out to on the Fall River dock in 1915 was Claude Sinclair Tucker. He was born on February 3, 1891, in Lincoln, Rhode Island, and found his calling to live the life of a mariner at an early age. He did this in the tradition of many seafarers before him—he simply decided that farm work was just not for him.

Clair, as he was called, was the younger of two sons born to Atwell and Mary Tucker. He had no sisters. Before long, the family moved to nearby North Providence and then, in 1900, to Portsmouth, Rhode Island. Here Atwell, a practical famer, worked as caretaker for the town's sixty-acre poor farm. The Portsmouth poor farm housed older people and handicapped adults incapable of supporting themselves or maintaining a home. It was located on the current site of Raytheon Company in Lawton's Valley, an area between Narragansett Bay on the west and what is now Route 138 on the east.

As was the custom of the day, young Clair was expected to help out on the farm. Though his father did pay him, Clair was known to try to get out of plowing the fields by telling his father he had to stop because he had run over a nest of bees in the ground and the bees had stung the horses.

To diversify his career and income options, Clair also tried his hand at a number of profit-seeking ventures. One was beekeeping. He built hives and raised swarms of bees, which he sold for honey or pollination. One day an orchard owner needed a swarm and offered his old, working catboat with its wide rails in trade for the bees. The young entrepreneur agreed, deciding he could turn a dollar with the boat.

Clair Tucker and his dog at the Portsmouth Poor Farm, Rhode Island. Early 1900s.
Collection of Donald F. Tucker.

Clair began learning to sail. Before long, he was taking his cousins and friends out fishing and for just plain fun. At the time, Clair had a pet lamb. The lamb also loved to sail and would sit up on the rail of the catboat as they made their way along the waters off Portsmouth. When the catboat would come about and rail and lamb would tilt down close to the water, the lamb would instinctively run up to the high side of the boat.

Clair loved the catboat and loved to sail. Soon farming, bees, school and everything else took a back seat. The old catboat had become the catalyst for a long and happy relationship between a man and the sea.

OYSTERS GREW IN THEIR BACKYARD

Like the lobster of today, the oyster ruled the culinary waves of seafood during the era of Clair Tucker's youth. As historian John M. Kochiss wrote in *Oystering from New York to Boston,*

> *It is difficult for New Englanders and even New Yorkers to imagine oysters as the chief fishery product of the United States and the most extensively eaten of all shellfish. Yet at the turn of the century and before, the oyster was indeed king. Everyone, especially those living along the shore, knew all about this wholesome, nutritious bivalve and the multimillion dollar industry it spawned.*

Hundreds of acres of oyster beds lay right off the beach of the Portsmouth Poor Farm. With only an open lot and the railroad tracks separating the Tucker house and the shoreline, it was inevitable that Clair, by now in his mid-teens, would be one of those people familiar with the oyster industry and the people who pursued it right in his own backyard. Accordingly, his first job was as a watchman on the oyster beds situated off his beach. This first employment experience outside the family was the entrance into an industry that would be a part of his life for two decades or more.

The Native Americans and early colonial settlers found vast beds of oysters in the numerous inlets and bays of the region. The industry grew so much that early governing bodies found it necessary to try to preserve the abundance by limiting the taking of oysters. But by the early 1800s, demand for the bivalve outpaced the dwindling natural supply. Besides the oyster's obvious use as food, people used oyster shells as a material with which to build roads and as a source of lime for masonry work.

Fishermen in New England harvested from the inshore waters of New York, Connecticut, Rhode Island and Massachusetts where the salinity, temperature, food supply and bottom provided favorable conditions for oyster reproduction and growth. Using hand, rake, tong and dredge, they supplied "the fancy oyster preparations at the countless oyster bars, bays, saloons, houses, and cellars of New York, Boston, and Providence," wrote historian Kochiss. Between 1880 and 1920, production ranged from about twelve million to fifty million pounds of meat per year.

The route from the oyster's watery home to the dinner table was not always a direct one, however. To maintain their supply, oystermen used several techniques to artificially propagate the crop.

One technique was cultivation. Aided by a law that provided an exclusive right to propagate oysters in an area of underwater territory, the oysterman staked out his area of oyster beds in shallow waters. He marked it with floating, upright bamboo poles, and prepared the ground to provide a hospitable substrate.

Here, either free-swimming oyster larvae could settle or the oysterman could deposit seed oysters he had purchased or harvested elsewhere. When the crop matured, the oystermen simply dredged up the oysters and had them transported via coastal schooner to market or to new beds for even further growth underwater.

Some Long Island Sound oysters grew in areas that produced an inferior product, appearing tinted. Before going to market, the oysterman transferred these bivalves via coasting schooner to choice waters to the east. Often, the destination for these oysters was the oyster beds of Wellfleet or Cotuit on Cape Cod or Narragansett Bay. At these locations, they could "fatten," or increase in size, quality and flavor, and purify themselves, if necessary, before they were harvested for the final time.

THE YOUNG WATCHMAN

The companies that owned the oyster beds situated off the Portsmouth Poor Farm property hired watchmen, all known to Clair Tucker, who lived on boats that they used to guard the companies' underwater investments from poachers.

Clair would often walk the beach on the morning after any kind of a heavy breeze, just to see what had washed in. One such morning, he saw the overturned skiff that belonged to one of the watchmen. He surmised that the man had drowned. Later that day, when an oyster steamer came to work on the grounds, Clair reported what he thought had happened.

After what was likely a period of somber reflection, the thoughts of the man on the oyster steamer turned to practicalities, and he said, "I don't know what to do. I've got to have a watchman."

Clair spoke up, "I'll take the job."

The man laughed and said, "Pretty young, aren't you?"

"I can do the job."

After a while, the oyster man said, "I'll tell you what I'll do. I'll give you the watchman's job until I can get in touch with the office in New Haven, and they can do what they want to."

With that, Clair looked forward to reporting for work in a maritime capacity for the first time. His pay was three dollars a night, which he considered big money.

Within a few days, he faced his first test when poachers in a large powerboat towing three big skiffs motored in and anchored. Two men jumped into a skiff and quickly began tonging for oysters. Clair was scared to death.

He nevertheless jumped into his own skiff and rowed out to them. They were the hardest-looking gang he had ever seen, and he was ready to pull for shore.

"What the hell you guys doin' here?" he hollered.

"We're tongin' oysters."

"You're on H.C. Rowe and Company's grounds."

"No, we're not."

"Yes, you are."

With Clair still scared to death, the poachers soon departed. Luckily, he had rowed by the stern of their vessel to get her name.

"Oh, we know that boat. We've had a lot of trouble with them," the company said when Clair reported the incident.

Clair continued his work as a watchman until the company notified him by mail that it would be replacing him and its other watchmen with big powerboats carrying big powerful searchlights. Apparently, the company had liked his work, though, because it thanked him for all his efforts and continued to give him twenty dollars a month just to keep an eye on the grounds.

ABOARD A NAVY TUGBOAT: EPISODE ONE

As the twentieth century approached, the U.S. Navy grew in size and importance. Gone were the wind-powered sailing vessels of old. Ships with steam-driven engines fueled by coal now served the nation. This meant that the navy needed huge quantities of that commodity and portside facilities, called coaling stations, that could supply its battleships and cruisers. One of the navy's largest coaling stations was established at Melville just before the turn of the century. It was located less than a mile north of the Portsmouth Poor Farm and opposite Prudence Island. Here, a tugboat towed barges loaded with coal to the ships anchored right off the station.

Clair Tucker knew the captain of the tug and a lot of the gang there, and as he was no longer working as watchman on the oyster beds, he decided to take a walk up there and visit.

"Hey, we want a deck hand on here. You want the job?" the skipper asked.

"I'd never been working on any kind of a craft, so to go on the tugboat was a big deal," he remembered years later. But soon, Clair began an eighteen-month stint on the towboat.

"It was an eight-hour day. Six days in the winter, and five, I think, in the summer…I got $1.52 for an eight-hour day, and no overtime. Sometimes if they were sure they wasn't going to use the boat that day, they would give us the afternoon off or something to pay us for overtime."

With the twenty dollars a month he made from the oyster company and his pay as a deck hand, Clair was beginning to accumulate a little bit of money.

THE *MOAMA*

Maybe it was wanderlust, for Clair Tucker surely wasn't seeing the world by motoring around the coaling station waters. Things were going well on the tug, but after eighteen months he took one look at the great three-masted schooners loading lumber in Fall River and decided to move on to bigger and better things.

On that day, Clair jumped a train as it passed by the poor farm, getting off within walking distance of Cook Borden and Company, just north of Battleship Cove today. Clair found out that the skipper of one of the three-masters, the *Moama*, was a man short in the fo'c'sle.

"Well, I look at them big spars and everything and it looks like a big deal, you know. He was going to South Amboy, New Jersey, to load coal for Saint

John, New Brunswick. And I thought just for a vacation, for a change of scenery, or something, I'll ship with him," he later explained. In addition to Clair, a couple of other young men signed on.

The *Moama* wouldn't be shoving off for a few days, so Clair and his pals thought they'd like to go ashore for the evening around Fall River. Because they would only get paid when they reached Saint John, they went aft and asked the skipper for a little spending money.

"Alright," he said and then counted out only twenty-five cents apiece for the three of them. But when that happened several nights in a row, he stopped them with a promise: "Hey, you fellas are drawin' too much money. I tell you what I'll do. I won't give you no more money until we get to South Amboy. When we get there, I'll give you money. You can go over to New York and have a good time for yourselves." New York! None of them had ever been to New York. The excitement was too much, and until they got there, that's all they talked about.

Eventually, the *Moama* made South Amboy. After supper, they got shaved and dolled up as best they could and went aft to get their money to go into town. This time the captain counted out seventy-five cents apiece—only seventy-five cents to go in to New York and have a big night for themselves.

Once under way again, the schooner was towed from South Amboy up and out through the Hell Gate and sailed as far up as New Haven, where the winter-like weather delayed them a few days. The *Moama* proceeded east to New London and found the harbor filled with so many vessels that there was scarcely a place to anchor. Again, they waited a number of days.

Finally, there came a nor'wester, and everybody started getting under way. The *Moama* was the last to leave the harbor, however. Unlike many of her contemporaries, the *Moama* was a still a "hand puller"—that is, she did not have a small engine called a "donkey engine" to help with the sails and the anchors. Because it took so long for the crew to manually raise the sails and pump the windlass to raise the anchors, there was hardly a schooner left in sight by the time the *Moama* got under way.

The *Moama* got down into Vineyard Sound at sunset, and the wind faded out with the sun. The tide was making a head, so they ran into Tarpaulin Cove and anchored. In the morning, the captain decided to get under way and go over among the fleet of big four- and five-masters out in Vineyard Sound. Even more vessels lay up ahead. "In Vineyard Haven Harbor was a million or more—packed full. You never saw such a fleet of vessels!" Clair Tucker later reminisced.

Before long, the captain of the *Moama* began to consider setting sail again and trying to make it around Cape Cod. Clair began to get concerned. Because the sandy bottom of the waters off the Cape could shift unpredictably, the journey around the Cape was often dangerous. Besides, Clair didn't see any of the newer, sturdier vessels in the harbor making a move. Nevertheless, the *Moama* got under way. "It was slow goin', but we got out around the Cape. I don't know how the hell we ever did it," he said.

Once past this hurdle, the *Moama* got into a calm for a couple of days before resuming her journey to Saint John. Just as she sighted Boon Island, the wind busted out northeast and with it, a snowfall. Running back into Kittery, Maine, she anchored behind the breakwater. Laying over a few days seemed to be becoming an unavoidable occurrence.

Clair recalled how much the weather affected their journey:

> *It was cold as blazes there. We froze in enough so as you couldn't get through it with a row boat. We laid there several days. It was blowin' like hell the whole time. Oh, it was a bad spell. Finally, we got a chance. My God, we went out and we made kind of a slow passage down to the Bay of Fundy, but we never stopped anywhere along the line. Then, by Jesus, we had one bad day there. Southerly. Rough as hell.*

The stop-and-go voyage continued. On one occasion, they lost the wind, and the crew had to go aloft to furl the topsails to keep them from whipping about. Clair remembered a lesson he had learned earlier in the voyage, and it helped him to not get stuck this time working on the most difficult sail. Earlier in the trip, when Clair was literally still learning the ropes, the captain called on the crew to set the topsails. One of Clair's fellow crew members jumped for the main, and another went for the spanker. That left Clair with the fore topsail. He got the job done, but he found out the hard way that it was the most difficult sail of the three.

As the end of his first voyage neared, Clair was stationed at the helm. Freezing and no doubt fatigued, his two hours at the wheel were supposed to be up. When his watch mate walked aft to relieve Clair, the skipper unexpectedly ordered the mate to go up forward again. When the captain commands, you can't ask questions, and so the cold and curious first-timer from Portsmouth remained at the wheel.

The schooner was soon at anchor in the harbor. When the anchor was down, Clair let go of the wheel and went to help the others furl what short sail they had on her. But before he could, the captain said, "You stay here." Clair remained aft by the wheel while his mates were finishing up the work.

The captain then turned to Clair and declared, "There, now, when you get home, you can tell the folks that you steered a vessel into Saint John Harbor."

Clair had to thank him for the honor, but, by God, was he cold!

They eventually struck the topmasts to go under the bridge and over the Reversing Falls. When they got everything shipshape, the skipper called Clair and his pals in and paid them off, as agreed upon. The captain then offered to keep them on.

"I got a charter to go to Fredericton and load lath for New York," said the captain. "Now, if you stay aboard the vessel and go up to Fredericton and look after her, I'll pay you while we get loaded and ready to go, and then I'll sign you on."

"I want to go home to go lobsterin' next summer," Clair said.

"Too early to go lobsterin'," the captain protested. "When it comes time, I'll pay you off any place we happen to be."

Clair hated to disappoint him, but he couldn't see staying in that temperature-challenged country any longer. He boarded the first steamer for Boston and headed for the shipping office. A couple of days went by without any work opening up. "I haven't been home in quite a while," Clair thought to himself and then took the train back down to his parents' home in Portsmouth.

He later took a job as a quartermaster at the helm of an oyster steamer.

Aboard a Navy Tugboat: Episode Two

One day Clair again went up to the coaling station to see the gang. Down at the dock where the towboat was tied up, he ran into the skipper.

"Hey, your old job's open on the towboat here," the skipper said. "You want it? They're payin' more money."

"Yeah, how much?"

"They're payin' two dollars a day now."

"I don't think so. I'll think it over."

"Damned, if I didn't ship on her," Tucker later recalled, "and I stayed on her again for eighteen months!"

CHAPTER 5

The Newport Years

THE TOUR

One day in 1915, Sinclair Tucker decided to jump the train that ran near his house and ride north into Fall River. He stopped at the dock of the Cook Borden lumber company, where he saw the *Coral* being loaded with lumber. He knew the *Coral*'s captain and owner, Irving D. Talbot, who had part-ownership in a cottage on the shore next to his family. As he approached the *Coral*, Clair saw that, for some reason, Captain Talbot had reached a point of frustration and that the *Coral*'s load of lumber bound for Block Island was the straw that was breaking the camel's back. As Clair got within hearing distance, the captain called out, "Tucker, you want to buy a boat?" The thing was that Captain Talbot really meant it.

Young Clair wasn't quite sure—this was all pretty sudden. He *did* have quite a bit of experience on small vessels and had even gone aboard that three-master carrying coal to New Brunswick. So, to keep the possibility under consideration and to make a quick inspection of all the gear and rigging and equipment and such, Clair took the captain up on his offer to tour the vessel.

Anyone standing on the dock, Clair included, could see that the *Coral*'s hull was painted the traditional dark green with the rails trimmed in white. The bowsprit, sticking out from the bow of the schooner, was also dark green except for a foot or two of white paint at the end. White paint also marked the ends of the two spars (the rounded lengths of wood at the top and bottom of the sail) on each mast, the gaff on top and the boom on

Old Harbor, Block Island, Rhode Island. The *Coral* is in the left center of the photograph. Late 1800s. *Collection of Donald F. Tucker.*

the bottom. Like the two masts, though, the remainder of each spar was not painted but instead coated with a clear preservative, a sort of paint-like shellac. Together, the mast and spars provided the structure supporting each of the canvas fore-and-aft sails. A topsail attached to an extension above each mast provided additional sail area.

Trailboards added decoration on either side of the hull. The black trailboards were indeed boards, painted white at the top and bottom and adorned with gold-leafed carvings. The only thing they trailed, however, was the far end of the bowsprit, as they sat a foot or so beneath the rails at the bow of the vessel.

Built into the hull on both sides, between each rail and trailboard, was the hawse pipe. Not really a pipe, this oblong-shaped, cast iron–ringed opening in the hull provided a place for the heavy anchor chain to pass through as it attached to one of the *Coral*'s two anchors. The anchor itself was of the traditional sort, with a stock and flattened, pointed flukes. On the hull at the stern, white painted lettering proclaimed, CORAL NEWPORT RI, the schooner's port of enrollment.

But Clair was more concerned with what he would see above and below deck. If what he saw during his tour of the *Coral* had been written down for history, it likely would read like this:

THE CAPTAIN AND THE PROSPECTIVE CAPTAIN stepped aboard the *Coral* about midway between the bow and the stern. Directly before them was the main hatch, through which cargo destined below deck would be loaded. A thought ran though Clair's mind: "This is a small vessel, and we'll need all the cargo space we can get."

They walked toward the bow over the wide wooden planks. Situated right in front of the foremast and bolted securely to the deck lay the windlass, sometimes called a winch. They saw the heavy anchor chains wrapped around both ends of this low-lying cylinder whenever the anchors were raised closer and closer to the surface of the water. Even Clair knew that it was easiest if both the captain and a mate took to the up-and-down, see-saw-like pumping operation that made the windlass revolve.

Captain Talbot then led Clair to the forward hatch, on the port (left) side of the foremast, and they descended into the fo'c'sle. Under the bow, on either side were the chain lockers and, between them, the paint locker. The captain pointed to the bunks on either side. "Old Nick, my mate, uses one of 'em. He can work for you, if you should decide to keep him on," he explained. Then he added, "It might be a good idea to keep him on."

The *Coral* foredeck with the port anchor catted. The windlass is in the center of the photo. *Collection of Donald F. Tucker.*

They began to walk toward the stern. Instead of a flat flooring to walk on, the walls and floor below deck were as if one piece, rounded in the shape of the hull beneath it. It doesn't seem to make sense, but this rounded floor and sides were called the "ceiling," perhaps because they were considered to be a top layer attached to the ribs and hull planking below.

As Captain Talbot and Clair walked aft, they next saw the foremast extending through the main deck and into the footing in the hull. This was where the anchor chains terminated following a few winds around the windlass on the deck above.

Continuing toward the stern, the main hold lay before them. This was where the cargo was stored below deck. "The guys loading and unloading will see a lot of the main hold," Clair mused.

The main hold was separated into port and starboard sides by the centerboard trunk, which surrounded the centerboard. The centerboard was a type of moveable keel that could be lowered through the hull into the water. Doing this helped counteract the vessel's tendency to slip sideways as it sailed.

A little farther on, Clair saw the two bunks of the main cabin attached to either side of the hull. A third bunk ran from side to side beneath the ladder to the main deck. Above the side bunks, on the main deck, sat the after hatch, a raised structure about a foot high. "Windows in the sides of the after hatch will let in some much-needed daylight," thought Clair as he looked up.

They continued walking aft below deck, and they could see and smell the cast-iron, wood-burning stove. In Clair's mind, this would be a welcome spot when the weather started to take on a chill.

They finally ascended the ladder's four steps back up to the main deck. Forward of the aft hatch was the hand pump. Clair really didn't want to think about pumping out the bilge water that was sloshing around down below among the ribs. Instead, he stepped up about a half a foot onto the quarterdeck. He eyed the wooden water barrel, covered over the top with canvas, with a tin cup and a porcelain mug hanging off the side. "Water for a summer's day," he thought.

Clair then turned to face forward. He stood on the quarterdeck at the helm. The twenty-four-year-old placed his hands on the wheel and fixed his sights beyond the masts, beyond the bowsprit and out into the water. It isn't too much to imagine that at that moment, Clair drifted into a daydream of the new direction that his life's voyage might be about to take.

Captain Tucker on the quarterdeck of the *Coral* in Nantucket. Note the planks, laid on the deck for protection when loading and unloading. 1934. *Collection of Donald F. Tucker.*

BEFORE LONG, CAPTAIN TALBOT and Clair agreed to a price—$2,000. In addition, Captain Talbot would see to it that Clair got enough work hauling oysters so that he could pay for the vessel by fall. Clair would own a six-eighth share in the *Coral* while Mrs. Josephine Craw of Rowayton, Connecticut, a shareholder, would own the remaining two-eighths.

CAP FINDS HIS MATE

For about the first six or seven years after purchasing the *Coral* in 1915, Captain "Cap" Tucker mostly hauled lumber, building materials and oysters. He usually carried lumber and building materials from Fall River to the islands in Narragansett Bay for new construction. Cap also ventured to Long Island Sound to load oysters for Warren and Bristol, Rhode Island, and Cotuit, on the southern shore of Cape Cod. His trips to Cotuit were his only forays to the east of Fall River at the time.

To a lesser extent, he hauled other cargoes at this time—brick from Connecticut and cordwood from Assonet. He delivered the cordwood, mostly pine, to Newport.

When not delivering a cargo, the *Coral* could be found in Newport, Rhode Island, the port whose name graced the *Coral*'s transom. After all, Newport was only about five miles south of Captain Tucker's home at the poor farm, where he still lived with his father and mother. Newport Harbor also offered the advantage of being relatively free of freeze ups during the winter months.

In the early years, Cap kept the *Coral* in operation year-round. He worked the schooner throughout the winter, except when he felt there was danger of being iced in. If a harbor or port was not iced in and a charter was available, he'd take the charter.

Schooner work often brought Cap to the Fall River area. It was here that he met Catherine Sullivan. The young couple married in the spring of 1917. There is no known record of Cap carrying his bride over the threshold, but if he did indeed do so, he had to have been creative because the schooner was their home during that first summer. Their "address" was a dock in Newport Harbor. They took over the main cabin, relocating Nick forward to the fo'c'sle.

The newlyweds had to make do with tight quarters, for the *Coral* was small by schooner standards. Cap loved the little *Coral*, and he used the vessel's size to his advantage. When carrying cargo, time spent idling at the dock was money, and the smallness of the vessel allowed Cap to load and unload more quickly and make more trips.

Five months later, the Tuckers found an apartment in Fall River, not far from the apartment of Mrs. Tucker's parents. Two of their children were born in Fall River: Bill in 1919 and Helen in 1920.

LUMBER FROM THE SPINDLE CITY

In the early years, Captain Tucker hauled many loads of lumber and building materials originating from a major lumber company, Cook Borden and Company of Fall River. The company provided lumber for most of the large textile and manufacturing companies in Fall River, as well as lumber and building materials for building houses.

Cook Borden was located on Davol Street at the foot of what was then Turner Street. This strategically valuable location made it possible for the company to easily receive shipments by either water or land. Lumber from Maine and the southern states arrived by large schooners at the Cook Borden dock on the Taunton River just to the west and by railroad just to the

Schooners loading at the Cook Borden and Company lumberyard, Fall River. *Courtesy of Philip Arthur Hartley III.*

east. Smaller schooners or local rail then transported the lumber to smaller distributors or to the work site.

In 1910, just five years before Captain Tucker purchased the *Coral*, delivery by motor truck took the place of delivery by horse, and Cook Borden began to carry building materials other than lumber. This development was good for the building contractors, and they accounted for a significant amount of the Cook Borden's sales. It was good for Captain Tucker, also, due to the many new construction projects on the islands and shore communities of Narragansett Bay.

For some of these projects, Cap began hauling a unique type of cargo—entire houses. Using plans supplied by the builder, estimators at Cook Borden listed all the materials necessary to build a house. The yard workers gathered the materials and loaded them onto a schooner, such as the *Coral*. When the schooner reached her destination, workers off-loaded the material and transported it, usually by horse and wagon, to the job site.

Captain Tucker could always get a charter to deliver for Cook Borden because the foremen and workers got to know him as a reliable and likeable schooner man. In an interview later in life, Cap recalled the trip that cemented his reputation there. Here is the story:

THE OLD SUPERINTENDENT at Cook Borden's came down to the dock all worked up.

"Oh, my God. I don't know what you're goin' to do. You'll be froze in solid, come mornin'."

Cap knew exactly what the superintendent meant. It was wicked weather, he thought to himself, cold and blowin' a half a gale of wind. On a night such as this, Fall River could freeze over. Cap would much rather be in Newport where he kept the *Coral* in winter, where there was little chance of the harbor water freezing the *Coral* in.

But here he was at the Fall River dock, where at six o'clock on a winter's night, the yard workers had finally finished loading the *Coral*. She was bound for Jamestown, farther down the bay, with all the unassembled components, even down to the nails, that would soon become a house. Cap had carried some loads for the lumber company before, so he knew that getting frozen in at the dock with this load would cause a problem for them. Delivering the load tonight, on the other hand, could mean more work from Cook Borden in the future.

This would be a solo trip. Cap had no help aboard at the time and didn't know where to get anyone. In spite of this, he shoved off with the help of the yard workers. With the wind blowing mightily from the nor'east, he continued on his way, alone under short sail. Eventually, as he approached his destination, he thought to himself, "Goin' to be too rough for me to lay in at the dock where I need to unload." So he swung off and went into Newport to tie up.

Because he hadn't had supper, he went ashore to find a restaurant. As he walked up the street, he saw one of the thermometers that some of the stores would hang up in front. He stopped and looked at it. It was three below zero.

"I looked at that foolish thermometer," Cap recalled, "and I began to shiver and shake to beat the band. I didn't feel a bit cold until I looked at that. In my concern to get into port, I'd forgotten just how cold it was."

The next day, the wind shifted, and he was able to deliver the cargo over to Jamestown. His fortunes shifted, too, since he would soon secure more of the cargoes from Cook Borden that he had sought.

Captain Tucker aboard the *Coral*. Date and location unknown. *Collection of Donald F. Tucker.*

As TIME WENT ON, Cap developed a good sense of his limits and a respect for the waters and weather conditions facing him. These characteristics kept the *Coral* and her skipper free of mishap throughout the years. One example of this occurred during an especially cold part of the year. A three-master was making her way from Down East to Cook Borden's in Fall River. The schooner anchored near Sandwich at the east end of the Cape Cod Canal. A tugboat then picked her up and towed her through the canal to Buzzards Bay. The *Moama* anchored in the bay with several other schooners, as was typical, waiting for a fair wind. But ice formed around the vessels before the wind rose up, and the group of schooners froze in solid.

When at last the ice broke up, it remained in great floes, one of which dragged the three-master southward. Then, the tide caught the trapped schooner, transporting her into the turbulent waters of Woods Hole, where she fetched up on the ledges and filled with water.

The old superintendent at Cook Borden wanted Captain Tucker to go to Woods Hole, off-load the lumber from the immobilized schooner and bring the cargo to the yard in Fall River. Declining Cook Borden's offer, Cap recalled years later, "I didn't know much about Woods Hole at the time. Only that it was a tough place, and I wouldn't go." In a strange twist of fate, the three-master disabled in Woods Hole was the *Moama*, the first schooner Cap ever sailed aboard.

OYSTERS FROM LONG ISLAND SOUND

By the time Captain Tucker purchased the *Coral* in 1915, oysters had become a household word in New York and New England. The work of freighting what scientists called the American or Eastern oyster (*Crassostrea virginica*) would provide Cap with a steady income for many years to come. Even during the 1920s and '30s, when the amount of oyster harvesting and propagation declined somewhat, he could easily find a load of oysters to transport.

As a schooner man, Captain Tucker's role in the oyster trade was critical. His job was to transport live shellfish to their destination and keep them in good condition while doing so. He would take a load of oysters that had

The *Alice S. Wentworth* at Nantucket with a load of quahog shells to be used for making driveways. 1930s. *Collection of Donald F. Tucker.*

been harvested from Long Island Sound and haul them eastward to oyster beds in Narragansett Bay or to Cotuit on Cape Cod. Here, workers would shovel the oysters overboard so that they would settle on the oyster beds at the bottom. By transplanting mature oysters to these choice waters during the season before going to market, the quality of the final product would increase and thus command a higher price.

Captain Tucker usually carried his cargo of 1,500 bushels of oysters on deck. When loading oysters on the *Coral*, the bushel baskets of the bivalves were slid down on planks from an oyster steamer and dumped on deck, then covered with canvas and kept wet. The owners of the oysters wanted the schoonermen to sail once their vessel was loaded. If the weather was bad, Captain Tucker would temporarily take shelter en route, often among the Thimble Islands or the breakwaters at Duck Island, both east of New Haven. When the *Coral* arrived at her destination, men came aboard and shoveled the oysters off the schooner as she traveled in an expanding square pattern. To create this pattern, Captain Tucker changed course ninety degrees at increasingly longer intervals.

Over the years he would haul load after load of oysters to the Goulds of Chatham, the Eldridges of Cotuit, Besse in Onset and his good friend Bill Shephard of Bristol, Rhode Island.

Cordwood from Assonet

One of Cap's favorite cargoes was one that was always in demand: cordwood. When the square section of the wood in the interior of a tree trunk was taken for lumber, slabs of wood from the outside of the trunk remained. These slabs had one rounded side and one flat side and were used as fuel for heating and cooking. Because of the widespread use of cordwood, Captain Tucker could usually find a load to haul in between other charters.

The term "cordwood" derives from the unit of measure by which the wood was sold. When cut into four-foot lengths, the slabs would be stacked four feet high. Two of these stacks sitting side-by-side extended for eight feet. The resulting 128 cubic feet of wood was sold as a "cord."

At this point in his career, Captain Tucker hauled mostly pine from Assonet, Massachusetts. He carried many loads to the Newport Coal and Wood Company on Bowen's Wharf. It supplied the cordwood for some of the Newport mansions.

A steam tug and two schooners at Assonet Village. *Courtesy of the Freetown Historical Society.*

One of the hallmarks of the coasting schooner was that it could maneuver easily into small, shallow inlets along the coast. The width and the depth of the river as one approached Assonet Village, however, prevented even a coaster as small as the *Coral* from reaching and departing it by sailing. Schooner captains, then, had two options: run a line from their vessel to a yawl boat or dory ahead of it and row, or hire a steam tug to tow the schooner. Although it involved an expense, Cap opted for the steam tug.

At Assonet Village, horse and wagons hauled the cordwood slabs to the dock, where they were dumped unceremoniously. When both the *Coral* and the cargo were ready, workers loaded twenty-eight to thirty cords by hand onto the vessel. First, the workers filled the hold below deck and then the remainder on deck as high as the boom would allow. To form a retaining wall on either side of the vessel, sideboards were set up above the rails. Each board was a twelve-foot long plank that was one inch thick and two feet wide. Several of these boards were stacked one on top of the other and lashed to galvanized pipes set into holes in the rail. Every available space was used, so much so that in order to get to the forward end of the schooner, the mate would need to climb over the top of the stacks.

Unloading cordwood simply required performing the same procedure in reverse. Unloading cargoes such as cordwood provided a little spending money for a transient person or someone out of work. Captain Tucker sometimes hired one or two to help out for the grand sum of twenty-five cents per hour. Some of the men would work for exactly one hour, then give someone else a chance. With quarter in hand, they'd head for the nearest tavern for food and drink. In those days, the bars provided a free lunch for their patrons. Typical fare featured soup, cold cuts, bread and pickles—nothing spectacular, but enough to fill an empty stomach. The worker's twenty-five cents got him a fifteen-cent shot of whiskey, a ten-cent beer chaser and the free lunch. Often, as the barkeep poured the shot, the patron wrapped his thumb and forefinger around the lip of the shot glass to get a little extra whiskey for his fifteen cents. This came to be known as the "sideboard shot."

BRICKS ACROSS THE SOUND

Brick was another important cargo for Captain Tucker. The *Coral* carried twenty-five thousand brick at a time between points in Long Island Sound and out to Fishers Island. Some people say twenty-five thousand "brick," while others say twenty-five thousand "bricks." Either way, the entire lot was loaded and unloaded by hand. If a man needed work and was strong enough to stack five or six bricks together and toss them as a unit from the dock to the deck of a schooner, or be on the receiving end to catch and stack them, then he was in luck. Unloading worked in reverse. The workers seldom bothered to use gloves—they were expensive and wore out too easily. Both the brickyard and the customer supplied the labor at either end of the trip.

UNNAMED MATE NUMBER ONE—THE *CORAL* ENCOUNTERS CATTLE

When Cap told a story in later years, he usually mentioned someone's name only if they were one of the steady crewmen or a schooner captain friend. Many others went unnamed such as this short-term mate.

Like many schooner captains, Captain Tucker would take any reasonable cargo available as well as any temporary mate who could do

Cattle aboard a sloop in the Bahamas. *Collection of Donald F. Tucker.*

the job. There was a navy man Cap knew who worked on an oil barge at the Melville coaling station. When Cap saw him one day, the navy man said, "I'm getting paid off here in a short while. How about me goin' with you on the schooner?" Cap figured the man would be okay, so he took him aboard.

The first job Cap and the new mate worked was a bit out of the ordinary, but Cap had done it before. Twice a year, a farmer contracted with him to transport his cattle from Bristol Ferry, Rhode Island, to Portsmouth, where he would put them to pasture. For this trip, he wanted to move pigs and hens that had been placed in cages in addition to ten cows.

Fortunately, the platform that rose up and down at the old ferry slip was in working order, and Cap was able to bring the *Coral* alongside to load. Though it was highly unusual for any of Captain Tucker's cargoes to ever complain, several of the cows let their thoughts be heard as each was led aboard, lasso style, and secured on deck.

For awhile, the trip to Portsmouth went swimmingly for Cap, the *Coral*, the cows and the cages. That all changed when one of the big steamboats out of Fall River came plowing by. Cap picks up the story from there:

The schooner started rollin' like hell in the steamer's wake! It was the spring of the year, and, by Jesus, those cows were so scared that they started off. There was crap all over the deck. What a hell of a mess!

We got over to Portsmouth, and we got 'em unloaded off there at the dock, crates and all. The Navy guy stands there lookin'. He says, "I didn't ship aboard here to play nursemaid to cows!"

We grabbed a couple of buckets and brooms. What a hell of a time we had swabbin' that deck!

We're not sure, but the navy man may have soon deserted.

OLD NICK

Schooners enjoyed the advantage of requiring few crewmen aboard to raise the sails, haul the anchor and accomplish the many other day-to-day tasks. Cap could sail alone, if necessary, and on occasion he did. But having the assistance of one mate worked best. Having to hire only one mate made things even better.

A coastal trip such as the ones the *Coral* would typically embark on lasted no more than a few days. Still, captain and mate had to get the job done and live amicably enough while doing it. Cap sometimes hired a mate short term. Over the years, though, Cap was fortunate in finding several who worked for extended periods. Old Nick, French Louie, George Gale and Ben Waterworth all had the right combination of what it took to make a good mate: knowledge, skill, experience, reliability, character, honesty and compatibility. The first of these longtimers was Old Nick.

When Captain Tucker bought the *Coral*, he inherited Old Nick, who had worked for Captain Talbot. He was an experienced schooner man, always having worked in nearby waters on smaller coasters, never sailing on deep water. For him, the *Coral* was a place to earn his living and a place to lay his head. He worked for a bunk in the fo'c'sle and for his grub, pipe tobacco and an occasional bottle of "cough medicine." When Cap was away, Nick was the unofficial watchman.

Like many sailors before him, Nick was also very superstitious. And so, Nick was some mad when Captain Tucker brought his new bride aboard to live. He considered it a bad omen to have a woman aboard a vessel, and he let Captain Tucker know about it. After a few weeks, however, he

Captain Tucker, left, and Old Nick. *Collection of Donald F. Tucker.*

Captain Tucker's binoculars. Cap always kept these handy aboard the *Coral*, just above the binnacle on the cabin rooftop. *Photograph by Robert Demanche.*

calmed down and conceded, "You know, Cap, it's not so bad having your wife aboard, and she certainly is a good cook!" Mrs. Tucker's "kitchen" was simple but adequate. She did her cooking on a wood-fired stove down in the main cabin. Above it was a shelf and a "Charlie Noble" pipe venting the smoke to the open atmosphere.

The *Coral* sailed at a time when cellphones, GPS, communications satellites, SONAR, LORAN, electronic depth finders and similar electronic gear did not exist. The *Coral* wasn't high tech. It wasn't low tech. With only charts, dividers, binoculars and a barometer, the *Coral* and other vessels of her day were essentially no-tech. Nick even considered the barometer to be unnecessary technology.

In Nick's view, barometers were unreliable and caused an overly cautious skipper to waste a lot of time in port or at anchor. But like his acceptance of Mrs. Tucker on board, he changed his outlook after one foul February night off Point Judith, Rhode Island.

Fortunately, Captain Tucker lived by the barometer. To the sailor, a rapid drop in the level of mercury inside this glass instrument indicated that bad weather was approaching. And on that night, drop it did. Cap steered the schooner behind a nearby breakwater and put out an extra anchor. Here the *Coral* safely rode out the severe storm when it arrived, just as Cap had predicted.

Caught in this same storm, Captain Zeb Tilton and the *Alice S. Wentworth* were not so lucky. Zeb was hauling a load of plumbing supplies and roofing shingles from New York to Vineyard Haven. The *Wentworth* made Point Judith but not the safety of the breakwater, instead suffering damage when she was driven ashore. When conditions improved, Captain Tucker helped get the *Wentworth* refloated by taking on some of her cargo to lighten her up.

A bit of Nick's tongue-in-cheek humor comes through in this story about wildlife communication, later recalled by Captain Tucker:

> *My God, that was a character for you. He was funny. We laughed more with that old guy! He'd keep you laughing all the time.*
>
> *You know what you call horse loons? Big loons? In the night, if it's calm, still, they make an awful screechin' noise. Oh, you can hear 'em a mile. So, we'd be going along at night sailing and you'd hear one of those screeches.*
>
> *Nick would say, "Did you hear that? Did you hear that, fella?"*
>
> *I'd say, "Yeah, what'd the loon say?"*
>
> *If we were coming east, Nick'd say the loon was saying, "Nor' east, nor' east," meaning that the wind was comin' from the no'th east. But, if we*

were turned around going the other way, Nick'd say the loon was hollerin',
"Sou' west, sou' west!"

Cap and Nick usually got along well, but there seems to have been at least one period of strained relations. We're not sure how long this went on, but apparently one day, things came to a head. Something made Nick decide to pack up and leave.

When Captain Tucker was in between charters during the winter, he would often go hunting and trapping. Some of his favorite spots were off Bulgarmarsh Road in nearby Tiverton and Westport. The Tuckers didn't own an automobile, but the trolley car could get him there just as well.

One day Cap caught a skunk and, boy, did it stink. So, being accommodating, Cap rode back with his prize on the outside of the trolley. As usual, he brought the skunk down to the *Coral* where he would cure the skin after first skinning the animal. He never got to the curing-the-skin part, though, because he accidentally slit the scent bag. The resulting stink overpowered whatever the waterfront smelled like on that particular day. Thinking little of it, Cap headed off.

Later, he went down to the schooner again and saw Old Nick with his suitcase walking up the street.

"Where're you going?" Cap called out.

Nick kept walking and didn't say a word.

He later told the men at the Cook Borden lumberyard, "That damn Tucker, if he didn't want me living aboard the vessel, he could have said so. He didn't have to do that!"

In time, both messes, the skunk and Old Nick's secure place aboard the *Coral*, were resolved. Nick continued to stay on until perhaps a few years after the Tuckers got married. His departure may simply have been prompted by some combination of old age and the Tuckers' decision to move from Fall River.

FRENCH LOUIE

We don't know much about French Louie, one of the *Coral* mates who served for an extended period of time. But we do know that he and Cap knew each other from the days when they both they both served as quartermasters on separate oyster freighters in Long Island Sound earlier in their careers. French Louie came aboard after Cap injured his back.

The injury occurred when Cap was working aboard the *Coral*, and it was serious enough to land him in a body cast at Massachusetts General Hospital in Boston. The itching and discomfort from the body cast drove him crazy, however, and there was little to relieve the situation. He put up with it as long as he could, but within forty-eight hours, with the irritation of the body cast and the thought in the back of his mind that he had to make a living, Cap convinced the doctors to cut the cast off. Returning to the schooner, Cap brought French Louie on to help but continued to work in much pain throughout the rest of his career.

In the days before automated, unmanned buoys and towers, there were numerous lightships stationed along the coast to mark underwater ledges, shallow water, shifting sands and other hazards to navigation. Lights were positioned high atop the masts of these vessels. After serving aboard the *Coral* for a few years, French Louie took a position as quartermaster on the *Azalea*. The *Azalea* was a lightship tender based in Woods Hole and was, like other vessels of her type, named after a flower. The lightship tenders maintained buoys and other aids to navigation as well as supplied and, at times, went to the aid of lightships and other vessels.

French Louie lived his last days at the U.S. Marine Hospital in Vineyard Haven on Martha's Vineyard. Institutions such as the marine hospital and similar "snug harbors" provided care and a home for naval, merchant and other seamen— among others—who were aged, infirm, poor or otherwise unable to care for themselves following their maritime careers. The U.S. Marine Hospital sat atop a hill above Lagoon Pond in Vineyard Haven where it commanded a view of both the pond and the harbor. A vessel lying in the harbor could set a signal that notified the hospital of a sick or injured sailor aboard. For many years it was a common sight to see the horse-drawn ambulance transporting a sailor from the wharf to the hospital. For a variety of reasons, the number of patients or residents in maritime homes declined as the years went by, and in 1952, the Health Service decommissioned the hospital. It later served as home to the St. Pierre School, a camp for youngsters, and is now owned by the Martha's Vineyard Museum.

Shorty Leach

Although Old Nick and French Louie were the longtime mates while the *Coral* was based in Newport, Captain Tucker also took on "medium-term" help from time to time. One of these mates, George "Shorty" Leach, stayed on for about a year. Early on, Cap hauled many loads of lumber and building materials for Cook Borden and Company of Fall River. Shorty Leach worked for Cook Borden, and it is there that he and Cap likely crossed paths. Following his time on the *Coral*, Leach worked at another Fall River lumber company, Prosser Lumber, and became a superintendent. While working at Prosser Lumber, he kept a summer home in Westport Point, where he owned a small place of business that sold Lyman boats and Evinrude outboards and kept the local anglers supplied with bait. In 1946, Captain Tucker's son Donald worked for Shorty for a summer and took away fond memories of setting crab pots, maintaining boats for rent, repairing motors and, yes, selling bait.

A Crewman from Virginia

On one occasion, Captain Tucker brought on a mate who learned very quickly but, unfortunately, didn't stay long. Little information was ever handed down about the man, except that Cap thought the world of him and that he returned to his family in Virginia.

Unnamed Mate Number Two—The Distracted Helmsman

Once, a contractor hired Captain Tucker to transport a load of lumber from Cook Borden's in Fall River to Jamestown, Rhode Island, on Conanicut Island where a lot of building was taking place. Cap, his temporary crewman, the contractor and three men the contractor sent down to do the work all sailed on the *Coral* to Jamestown. It made sense for them to hitch a ride on the schooner rather than pay the train and ferry fares to the island.

Cap let the temporary mate take the helm for awhile, a big mistake.

"I gave my mate the wheel, and he'd be talkin' with these guys. And the first thing you know, she'd be luffed up or somethin'," Cap later recalled about the sails flapping wildly as the *Coral* lost headway. "We had quite an argument. I was tryin' to keep him on the course. Finally, I had to give up all together and take the wheel for the rest of the way."

Not taking this very kindly, the mate announced, "When I get you on the dock, I'll fix you. I know better than to hit you aboard the vessel."

In time, the *Coral* reached the dock. As soon as she did, the contractor and his workers left. Cap stepped up onto the dock and told the mate that he'd tan his hide when he stepped off the vessel.

"Oh," the mate says, "I'm alright now. I got mad. But I'm alright now. Just give me my money and I'll go."

Cap continued to try to coax him up onto the dock, but the mate wouldn't budge. Finally, Cap figured that the stalemate with the mate wasn't worth it, gave him his money and never saw him again.

UNNAMED MATE NUMBER THREE—SLEEPING ON THE JOB

In this story, Captain Tucker felt compelled to cut one of his men loose, so to speak.

It seems that Cap had the mate row him ashore in the yawl boat so that he could pick up some grub and telephone around to try to find a charter. The captain said that he would holler from the dock when he wanted the mate to pick him up.

Before they left the *Coral*, however, Cap instructed the mate to perform some maintenance when the mate got back aboard the vessel.

So Captain Tucker went ashore to conduct his business. When he was through, he called out to the mate aboard the *Coral*.

No response.

He called out again.

No response.

That was funny, thought the captain. He knew that the mate had returned to the *Coral* because he could see the yawl boat laying off the stern.

Meanwhile, a young lad came rowing by the dock, and Cap hired the boy to take him and the grub out to the schooner. As they made their approach, Captain Tucker could see that the mate was sound asleep in a hammock the Captain had strung between the davits at the stern of the vessel. (The davits held the yawl boat when it was out of the water.)

Cap had the boy row him to the bow where Cap climbed aboard by way of the bobstays for the bowsprit. Seeing that the mate had not completed his assigned work, Cap proceeded to the stern where the mate was peacefully sleeping. Quietly, he took out his pocketknife and cut away the head rope on the hammock, sending the mate headfirst into the drink.

Captain Tucker expected the mate to resurface soon, but what seemed like minutes passed, and the mate did not appear. Captain Tucker now feared that he had drowned the fellow.

Finally, the mate came to the surface, covered in mud and spitting out water.

The mate was some mad, and once on board, he grabbed his gear and left as fast as he could.

Unnamed Mate Number Four—"Yawl Boats Are Scarce"

Both Captain Tucker and Bill Talbot recalled this story. Here's what happened:

One of the worst men Cap ever shipped as mate used to crew with Captain Irving Talbot, Bill Talbot's father, but somehow or other Cap shipped him.

The mate hadn't been aboard long when the *Coral* went into Greenport to load oysters. When the *Coral* came up out of Long Island Sound to Plum Gut in Gardiner's Bay, Cap saw two schooners also bound for Greenport, only a few miles away. Neither of the two schooners had an engine, but knowing that whoever got in first would get the charter for the oysters, Cap gave it all he had.

Greenport was crowded with vessels, so Cap decided to go in and find a hole to anchor. Getting hard onto the breakwater, he was thinking about taking the yawl boat ashore to get ahead of the other two boats. So, as Cap later recalled, "I guess the guy I had workin' had never been there before. We're tearin' in there and he's lookin' at the scenery. And I'm yellin' my head off, 'Get that headsail off of her.'"

Finally, the mate got it down off her, but Cap didn't have time to bawl him out. He lowered the boat, rowed ashore and signed up for the load of oysters. As he came out of the office, the captains of the other two schooners were coming in. That was how close it was.

When Cap was in such a hurry to get ashore, he didn't say anything to the crewman. But when he got back, he had plenty of time.

That evening, the captain of another schooner came by in his yawl boat and said to Captain Tucker, "I'm going ashore for awhile. Come on in with me." So, Cap jumped in his boat and went ashore, and they walked around town.

When Cap came back aboard, the yawl boat was gone, evidently taken by his crewman. Well, Cap figured, if a guy wanted to go ashore, it was alright with him—went ashore to get some rum, he guessed. So, Cap just turned in for the evening.

The next morning, Cap went to get the mate out of his bunk and found him soaking wet with all his clothes on. "What happened to you?" Captain Tucker asked.

"Well," he says, "When I was climbing from the yawl boat aboard the schooner, I fell overboard down between 'em."

"Where's the yawl boat?" Cap asked.

He says, "I swam and caught it. It's tied up astern."

"Well, suppose you hadn't caught it."

"I would have drowned."

"Well, that's all right. There's plenty of men around, but yawl boats are scarce."

That got him mad.

"I thought I'd seen some tough skippers on these schooners," the mate said, "but it didn't take me long to realize I hadn't seen anything till I shipped with you. I quit."

"You can't quit."

"Why not?"

"Because you was fired before you had a chance to quit."

The mate threw some things into a suitcase he had and went ashore.

Not long after, a fellow Cap knew came down the dock and said, "Got a job for me?"

"I suppose the guy who worked for me will be back lookin' for a chance for a ride back east," Cap said.

"No, he won't. You see that schooner goin' around the breakwater now?"

"Yeah, that's Talbot's schooner."

"I used to be on her, but now your man's on her. Your man and I was ashore together. *Talbot fired me.*"

WORLD WAR I

During World War I, coasters enjoyed somewhat of a resurgence. From the start of the war in early 1914, the United States remained neutral and stayed out of the fighting being waged in Europe. But by the spring of 1917, the sinking of American cargo and passenger ships by German submarines had helped propel the United States into taking up arms as part of the Allied effort with England, France and Russia. Tremendous demands to mobilize for the war were placed on the troops sent overseas. U.S. civilians back home also contributed significantly to the war effort.

One such civilian was Captain Tucker. When he received his draft notice, he dutifully made arrangements to tie up the *Coral* for the duration. At his induction physical in Newport, a member of the draft board spotted him and bellowed, "What the hell are you doing here?"

"What the hell does it look like?" came Captain Tucker's reply.

The draft board member admonished the young skipper for not knowing how vital his schooner was to the war effort, and he promptly sent Cap home. Cap was issued a "License to Navigate in Waters of U.S. Naval Districts," and for the remainder of the war, he hauled materials in Narragansett Bay to support the navy's operations in the Newport area.

UNNAMED MATE NUMBER FIVE—THE ROMANCE OF THE SEA

While doing work for the navy, Cap was allowed to take additional charters if time permitted. For one charter, he was hired to sail to Bridgeport, near Connecticut's western end, to pick up a load of oysters and haul it to Narragansett Bay. There were four or five men who used to hang around the dock in Newport who were always talking about wanting to go aboard the *Coral* with Captain Tucker. For this trip, Cap decided to take one of them, and the one he chose soon started bragging to the others, "Just imagine me. You fellas goin' to war, and I'll be sittin' here steerin' this schooner up and down the coast here. I feel sorry for you."

Cap and his new helper shoved off, and when they reached Bridgeport, two oyster boats, filled with bushel baskets of oysters that had been dredged from the bottom, came alongside the *Coral* on either side. Then a seemingly endless parade of bushel baskets filled with oysters, shells and all, were sent sliding down the planks from the oyster boats and onto the *Coral*. When they were through, some 1,500 bushels of oysters lay dumped on the deck of the *Coral*, ready for hauling. And the next thing to flop down on top of the oysters was Cap's exhausted new helper.

Cap couldn't get him up for some time, but the *Coral* had to sail. Cap told him that they had to get under way, so he finally complied.

Though now vertical, the hired hand still didn't have enough strength to help Cap hoist the sails. Eventually they made New Haven, but because the weather wasn't right, they anchored there in the harbor. Again, the helper flopped right down onto the deck. Now, even the opportunity for supper couldn't get him to move. At some point, he went below and crawled into his bunk.

When the *Coral* finally reached her destination in Narragansett Bay, the man told Captain Tucker that he had had enough.

"His nice summer's work was all finished," Cap later recalled. "By God, I've never forgotten that guy."

CHAPTER 6

A Convergence of Factors

During the mid-1920s, schooners carried their last important cargo, lumber, as part of the Florida building boom. But by this time, regular service by steam colliers had become commonplace. These colliers were steam vessels built specifically to carry coal, and they finished off much of the coastal trade formerly dominated by the larger, long-distance schooners. As better trucks and better roadways became more common, they, too, would help crowd out many of the remaining schooners.

There were changes in store for Captain Tucker and his family, also. Around the beginning of the 1920s, a convergence of factors prompted the Tuckers to move from Fall River to Fairhaven.

First, construction on Narragansett Bay had slowed, and far fewer charters of lumber and building materials were available from Cook Borden. Captain Tucker did, however, continue to haul an occasional load from there. He was also still hauling oysters from Long Island Sound, pine cordwood from Assonet and brick from Long Island Sound.

Second, Captain Tucker began to find steady work hauling cargo from additional ports on Buzzards Bay. One was cedar cordwood from Mattapoisett. The other was gasoline from New Bedford to the islanders on Nantucket.

Third, Captain Tucker installed a gasoline engine in the *Coral*. No longer would Cap and the *Coral* be solely reliant on the wind to get them where they were going. The engine would also help Cap maintain a reliable schedule for his runs to Nantucket.

Here is how cargoes, ports and the all-important gasoline engine prompted the Tuckers to consider moving from their Fall River home.

CORDWOOD FROM MATTAPOISETT

It all began one day when Cap was unloading pine slabs from Assonet at Newport Coal and Wood, where his Uncle Elmer Tucker was superintendent. Elmer Tucker was faced with a dilemma. He had to find another source of cordwood for his customers in the Newport mansions, only the wood couldn't produce too much smoke and it couldn't be sticky and messy to handle. Captain Tucker had a solution. Somewhere in his travels, he had learned that you could get cedar cordwood at Mattapoisett on Buzzards Bay.

Captain Tucker went on to haul many loads of cordwood from the Mattapoisett town pier to Newport and the islands over the years. Jerry

The *Coral*, in the foreground, loading cordwood in Mattapoisett. More cordwood lies stacked on the pier, just a few hundred feet from where the *Wanderer* was built. 1920. *Collection of Donald F. Tucker.*

Randall, Dennis Mahoney and Earl Tinkham provided much of this cordwood, and oxen hauled the heavy loads from forest to dock. A team of oxen moved slowly, so this method took quite a long time. But in the days when trucks were few and far between, each ox had the crucial advantage of being, well, strong as an ox.

The higher-quality cordwood headed for the Newport mansions meant that Captain Tucker could command a better price. When he took a charter to transport a cargo, he usually did not purchase the cargo from the provider, but because the Mattapoisett cordwood cargoes were bound for his uncle's coal and wood company, he made an exception.

GASOLINE FOR NANTUCKET

The island of Nantucket lies more than twenty miles to the southeast of Hyannis on Cape Cod and about fifty miles from New Bedford. In the years following World War I, much like it does now, the island depended on regular deliveries from off-island suppliers of all kinds. Although Nantucketers owned relatively few automobiles, gasoline powered the island's many scallop boats, quahog boats and other fishing vessels. A dealer on Nantucket who sold gasoline, oil, ice, wood and coal to the islanders was Captain Jack Killen.

One day, a piece in the newspaper caught Cap's eye. Captain Killen was looking for someone to haul gasoline to Nantucket while the vessel of his current gasoline hauler was undergoing repair. An enterprising Captain Tucker sent Captain Killen a letter, offering to run the gasoline charters for him. Killen replied that he would only be able to hire Captain Tucker temporarily until his other hauler was ready. That was good enough for Cap, who accepted and proceeded to provide reliable service. When the other vessel eventually returned to work, Captain Killen stayed with Cap and kept him as his regular supplier. It was a partnership that lasted until the *Coral*'s demise almost two decades later.

The gasoline that Cap hauled to Nantucket came in fifty-five-gallon metal barrels, hopefully already filled and waiting at the Socony (Standard Oil Company of New York) terminal when the *Coral* arrived there. The terminal was located on the south side of Fish Island in New Bedford, across the harbor from Fairhaven. Cap also picked up barrels of road oil for Nantucket at Fish Island. Additionally, Cap loaded road oil and paving oil in Fall River.

The *Coral*, just fallen off the wind and headed for Nantucket. Note the wake after coming about, ready for a fast sail from New Bedford. 1920s. *Collection of Donald F. Tucker.*

The *Coral* loading at Socony on Fish Island, New Bedford. *Collection of Donald F. Tucker.*

Workers rolled the barrels out on their sides on a raised track set on a pier. In the years before 1931, when he installed a donkey engine to help hoist the barrels from the dock to the deck, Cap would unlace the top of the foresail from the gaff, raise the gaff to the top of the mast and push the sail out of the way. A line ran from the deck to a block and tackle on the gaff, then down to the next barrel to be loaded. Here, the line attached to large metal tongs that were made fast to the top and the bottom of the barrel.

Many schooner captains at the time set up a slightly different configuration for hoisting. Unlike Captain Tucker, who used the foresail gaff, these captains carried a spare boom on deck, which they hoisted aloft to support the block and tackle. When not in use, the crew had to make sure the boom was secure on deck, as a loose boom rolling around could damage the vessel and endanger the crew.

When all two hundred or so barrels of gasoline were

Captain Tucker detached the foresail from the foresail gaff (on the left) and raised the gaff to use it as a hoisting boom. 1935. *Collection of Donald F. Tucker.*

loaded and arranged in such a way as to balance, or "trim," the schooner, the *Coral* headed for Nantucket. For a delivery to Nantucket, Cap charged $1 per barrel loaded with gasoline, and 15 cents for each empty returned, so his income for hauling a load of gasoline could be as much as $230.

The first barrels brought on board went below until the hold was filled, and the remainder was placed on deck. Once under way from New Bedford, the *Coral* would reach her point of delivery on Nantucket in seven to eight hours, according to *Log of the "Coral,"* a journal kept by *Coral* crewman George Gale.

Once, the *Coral* did even better. On August 11, 1925, Cap hauled 147 barrels of kerosene to Nantucket for M.F. Roache in only five hours and forty-

The *Coral* taking off a load of paving oil for road contractor John Ring at Old South Wharf, Nantucket. The truck sign reads, "J.A. Viera, Trucking, Furniture Moving." 1935. *Collection of Donald F. Tucker.*

five minutes. The trip is also noteworthy because this cargo was not gasoline, which Cap hauled there for more than fifteen years. Cap also occasionally carried paving oil from Fall River for John Ring's road construction work. Other occasional cargoes for Nantucket included road oil, which was applied to keep the dust down, from both New Bedford and Fall River and slabs of cordwood from Mattapoisett. Cap once transported furniture to the island for a Frenchman named Casey, possibly Fairhaven boatbuilder Majorique J. "Major" Casey.

Because Captain Tucker sometimes took a load of oysters, one might wonder whether the sharing of the same deck by oysters and gasoline on separate consecutive trips might cause health issues, either to the crew or to the oysters. This never seemed to be an issue. The oysters were just dumped on the open deck, shells and all. The gasoline, however, was contained in metal barrels, which sat on pine planks placed down on the deck to protect it from damage.

Smoking aboard a vessel carrying gasoline was another issue. Sailors in that era tended to smoke pipes or chew tobacco instead of smoking cigarettes because cigarettes would get wet easily. Captain Tucker allowed smoking on the *Coral*, and the captain himself smoked his pipe at the helm while fifteen to twenty barrels of gasoline sat nearby on the quarterdeck.

The gasoline barrels were fully sealed metal drums, he reasoned, and if any gasoline remained on top of a barrel after loading, it would have evaporated into the air. Besides, with the wind off the side of the vessel, embers were no problem. Cap may not have seemed concerned, but the captain's six-year-old son Donald spent the summer of 1938 aboard the Coral, and he was never really convinced.

THE LATHROP ENGINE

Time is money in many types of business, and the coasting trade was no exception. A schooner captain could lose the chance to haul a cargo if he wasn't in port when the cargo was ready to load. If he was in port, then he may have had to wait in line to get a space at the dock. He would then wait for workers to unload the cargo already onboard and load the new cargo. When loaded, the weather might delay his departure and, once departed, might delay or even prevent him from reaching his destination. Once in port, the process might begin again. These were issues that Captain Tucker and the Coral frequently faced.

The Coral's excellence as a sailing vessel contributed to Captain Tucker's success in the coasting trade. For about the first six years that Cap owned the schooner, however, he labored under two disadvantages. First, like many older coasters, the wind provided the only power to propel the Coral through the water. Second, the Coral was a "hand puller," that is, there was no "donkey engine," a small diesel engine up forward that helped hoist the sails, haul the anchor and load or unload cargoes.

The donkey engine would come in later years. Cap remedied the first disadvantage around 1920 at about the time he got the contract to haul gasoline to Nantucket. The wind may have been free of charge, but as the lifeline for anything on the island that required gasoline, Cap now needed the ability to sail whether there was sufficient wind or not. An auxiliary engine, powered by gasoline and designed for the marine environment, would provide that reliability. Maneuvering in tight spots would now be much easier, also.

Cap turned to the Lathrop Engine Company, located on the Mystic River in Mystic, Connecticut. It installed a twenty-eight-horsepower, four-cylinder, Lathrop engine in the stern of the Coral. The engine was built on a common base that had four individual blocks and pistons and a common crankshaft.

As mariners began to use this type of engine, they discovered that you could replace each of the seven-horsepower cylinders individually. Over time, Cap replaced two of the seven-horsepower cylinders with two ten-horsepower cylinders taken from a forty-horsepower Lathrop engine. In theory, this created a thirty-four-horsepower engine.

The *Coral*, looking aft from forward of the foremast. At this time, Captain Tucker had not yet installed the donkey engine. 1920s. *Collection of Donald F. Tucker.*

When Captain Tucker added engine power to the *Coral*'s sailing capabilities, he was in the company of many Connecticut lobstermen, who at the time were replacing their two-cycle engines with heavy-duty, four-cycle models. The marine gasoline engine itself was still a relatively new invention, having only been developed by the turn of the century to the point where large-scale production made commercial sense.

To reach the Lathrop Engine Company, the *Coral* passed through the soon-to-be-replaced swing bridge. After Lathrop installed the engine, the *Coral* again passed through the swing bridge, and Cap likely reveled in his schooner's new auxiliary power. The trip downstream was notable for another reason, however, as the *Coral* became the last sailing vessel to pass through that old swing bridge before its removal. About twenty years later, Cap would pass through the opened bascule bridge there on a different noteworthy voyage.

Some of Captain Tucker's customers still wanted pine cordwood, and the Lathrop engine made it much easier for him to get to and from Assonet—no more steam tugs required. The engine also opened up a new source for brick on the Taunton River: the Stiles & Hart Company in Taunton's Weir Village.

Brick from Taunton

After installing the new engine, Captain Tucker loaded and delivered many loads of brick at twenty-five thousand brick per load from the Stiles & Hart Company. As the brick was loaded, the vessel settled lower and lower into the fresh water of the river. On one occasion, one of the "mates" began to get quite anxious as he noticed that the water was nearly going over the rails and onto the deck. The mate, who was in fact Cap's young son Donald, was no more than six at the time, and he finally felt relieved when the *Coral* shoved off, and the vessel headed down river. As the salinity of the water increased, buoyancy increased, and the *Coral* gradually rose to her correct marks.

On the trip back down the Taunton River, Captain Tucker would need to pass through two drawbridges. One was a hand-operated affair controlled by the nearby blacksmith at Segreganset in Dighton. The other was the Slade's Ferry Bridge, which connected Fall River and Somerset. As Cap made his approach, he would need to blow his foghorn several times to get the drawbridge tender's attention.

When Captain Tucker traveled even farther south, down the Sakonnet River, he would also encounter the Old Stone Bridge between Portsmouth and Tiverton, Rhode Island.

CARGO NON GRATA

Far up into the Taunton River was Weir Village, home of the Glenwood Stove Company. The first Glenwood range was built in 1879, but even by then, Taunton had so many foundries that it was known as "The Stove City." Many people considered the Glenwood Stove Company to be the best of more than two thousand American stove makers that existed during some point in the 1800s.

Sand and clay were necessary to create the molds used to produce the steel grates and other parts of their stoves, and so the Glenwood foundry was a destination for schooners loaded with these two cargoes.

The *Alice S. Wentworth* unloading one hundred tons of soft coal (ninety-two tons on deck and eight tons in the after hatch to trim the vessel) for the two Nantucket schools. Circa 1938. *Collection of Donald F. Tucker.*

Bill Talbot recalled that one of these schooners was his father's vessel, the *George F. Carman*:

> *We also used to go up the Raritan River to Bloomfield, New Jersey, for clay. We'd go down light and bring back the clay. We also got sand from above Albany. We brought these up the Taunton River to the stove factories.*

As a successful schooner man, Captain Tucker could be somewhat selective in choosing the charters he wanted to handle. Sand and clay were cargoes he avoided. Vessels that did haul sand and clay used wheelbarrows or a bucket hopper, but the loading and unloading was more difficult and tedious than other cargoes, not to mention extremely messy. For similar reasons, coal fell into the same category as sand and clay as far as Captain Tucker was concerned.

Oysters

During the 1920s, Captain Tucker continued to find work freighting oysters. Years later, Bill Talbot recalled the extensive oyster business in Warren, Rhode Island, at that time. He had worked aboard the coasting schooners owned by his father, Captain Irving Talbot:

> *In 1921, my father made $2100 in 21 days runnin' oysters to Wellfleet and runnin' shells back. We used to pay $18 to go through the Canal loaded and $12 light.*
>
> *In the mornin', if you went over there to Warren, it'd be like a parade, all those oyster boats goin' down the bay. They used to be called oyster steamers, but they were propelled by gas motors.*

Some of the oyster boats and their owners in the Warren area included *Lola* and *Maria* (George Green Oyster Company), *Priscilla* (Blount), *Church* and *T.H.C.* (Warren Oyster), *Standard* (Smith Oyster Company), *Pearl Evans* and *Lola Crane* (Benny Rooks), *John B. Stuart* (R.R. Higgins) and *Beacon* (an unnamed Wickford, Rhode Island company).

CHAPTER 7

The New Neighborhood

B y around 1921, Captain Tucker had developed a steady source of available cargoes, and therefore income, centered on Buzzards Bay. Between hauling many loads of cedar cordwood from Mattapoisett to Newport and gasoline from New Bedford to Nantucket, it made sense for the family to relocate nearby. They moved to the town of Fairhaven, where they found a place to live at 82 Middle Street. The house no longer stands. Their third child, Frank, was born there in 1922. Several years later, they bought the house two doors to the south at 78 Middle, where two more children were born: Kathleen, also known as Dolly, in 1926, and Claude Jr., in 1928. Another baby died in childbirth.

Both homes were a stone's throw from New Bedford Harbor. The harbor connected the town with New Bedford, the great city of both whaling and later fishing, in ways that were related to work, heritage, geography and the economy.

A Long and Storied History

The community the Tuckers found at Fairhaven can boast a long and storied history, much of it maritime related. The list of noteworthy people and events associated with Fairhaven is extensive.

The pilgram John Cooke arrived on the *Mayflower* as a young boy in 1620. Nearly half a century later, he built his home and a garrison for protection in what is now the north part of Fairhaven.

In May 1775, one month after the battles of Concord and Lexington, two Fairhaven men and their followers set out from shore in a sloop and, off West Island, recaptured two American sloops taken by the British. A fort, later named Fort Fearing and then Fort Phoenix, saw action in 1778 during the revolution.

During the first half of the 1800s, at least five shipbuilding outfits operated in town. During the 1850s, the peak years of whaling, some fifty whaling vessels set out from this side of the harbor. One such whaleship, the *Acushnet*, departed Fairhaven in 1841 with a crew member named Herman Melville. His experiences aboard the whaler would influence *Moby-Dick*, published ten years later.

At least 130 native and adopted citizens of Fairhaven served as masters aboard whaling vessels between 1815 and 1882. To support the whaling trade, shore-side enterprises arose. "There were carpenter shops, sail and rigging lots, block-making shops, windlass manufactories and spar makers," wrote historian and newspaperman Everett S. Allen of Fairhaven. This list went on: a ship's bakery, spermaceti candle works, tryworks where whale oil was refined, a marine railway that hauled out vessels for repair and a windmill near Fort Phoenix that turned a grindstone that sharpened whaling tools. In the twentieth century, the shipyards in Fairhaven would greatly expand their services and reputation.

In 1841, the same year Melville shipped out of Fairhaven on a whaling voyage, Captain William H. Whitfield rescued several marooned fishermen, including a Japanese boy named Manjiro. Manjiro continued on to Fairhaven until the end of Captain Whitfield's voyage. Manjiro took well to his studies there and eventually returned to Japan, where he played a valuable role in opening Japan to the west.

Artist William Bradford, internationally renowned painter of sailing vessels and the Arctic climes, was born in Fairhaven in an area that is now part of the town of Acushnet. His home near Fort Phoenix still stands.

Joshua Slocum, master mariner and author of the classic book *Sailing Alone Around the World*, rebuilt an old oyster sloop at Oxford Village, also known as Poverty Point, in which he made his historic solo circumnavigation from 1895 to 1998.

During the Gilded Age, Henry Huttleston Rogers made his fortune with the Standard Oil Company. He was a close friend and financial savior of Mark Twain, oversaw the town's development and built the architectural gems one sees today—the Unitarian Memorial Church, Town Hall, Millicent Library and Fairhaven High School.

And, most recently, some local NFL fans have been known to turn the sound off when watching their favorite professional team play on TV. They prefer to hear the radio play-by-play called by the kid from Hawthorne Street who grew up to be the enthusiastic, authoritative and highly respected "Voice of the New England Patriots," Gil Santos.

Captain Tucker may never have met any of the celebrities mentioned above, but he did cross paths with many maritime people during his days in Fairhaven. Some of the following men were known nationally, some only locally, but all were interesting.

William Hand

William H. Hand Jr. was a nationally prominent naval architect, who, in 1920, purchased a property in Fairhaven at 80 Middle Street. Here, Hand established his design and boatbuilding business. In the early 1960s, U.S. Coast Guard Auxiliary Flotilla 65 formed the Acushnet River Safe Boating Club, which now owns the building at that address. Currently, a driveway sits just north of the building. A house sat on that spot in 1920, and within a year or so, Hand would have new neighbors there to rent the place—Captain Tucker and his family.

Hand's work in Fairhaven dates back at least to 1911, when the Fairhaven *Star* reported that he "rented the storehouse south of the old Atlas Tack factory and is building his V-bottom boats and hydroplanes there." Today, "the old Atlas Tack factory" still stands as part of Fairhaven Shipyard Companies' South Yard facility.

In 1922, Hand finished a pleasure boat that he built for Harry Rogers, son of Standard Oil tycoon and philanthropist Henry Huttleston Rogers of Fairhaven. The Fairhaven *Star* proclaimed her to be "without question the most expensive pleasure boat ever built in Fairhaven." This six-hundred-horsepower, sixty-five-foot mahogany vessel could reach a speed of twenty-seven to twenty-eight miles per hour. The newspaper further declared that "about every modern idea or appliance in connection with a boat" went into her making.

Although Hand was best known for his designs of V-bottom boats, he also designed motorsailers, schooners and nine other types of vessels. Working for Hand at one point or another at the 80 Middle Street site, which included construction and repair facilities, were boat designer Benjamin T. Dobson,

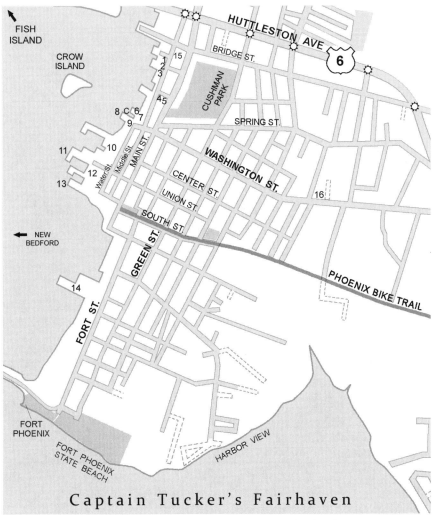

Captain Tucker's Fairhaven

1   1st home (open lot north of 80 Middle Street)
2   Wm. H. Hand, Jr. (US CGA) (80 Middle St.)
3   2nd home (78 Middle Street)
4   Park Garage
5   3rd home (84 Main Street)
6   Bones of the *Coral* (covered over with fill)
7   Taylor marine construction company
8   Delano's Wharf

9   Clifford Ashley's studio
10   Kelley's boatyard
11   Union Wharf
12   Casey's boatyard
13   Railroad Wharf
14   Peirce & Kilburn boatyard
15   4th home (97 Middle Street)
16   5th home (116 Washington Street)

C   Home of the *Coral*

Most of the Fairhaven sites in the story of Captain Tucker and the *Coral* were located along this one-mile stretch of shoreline. *Based on a map created by and courtesy of the Fairhaven Office of Tourism. Adapted by Robert Demanche.*

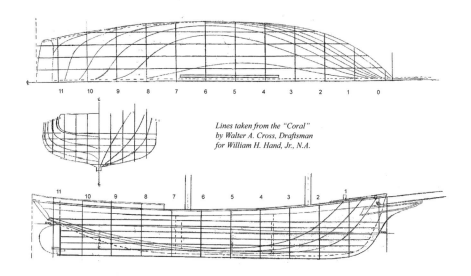

Offsets showing the lines of the hull of the *Coral*. *Courtesy of Barbara C. Whalen.*

draftsman and designer Richard O. Davis and boatbuilder Palmer Scott. A collection of more than two thousand Davis-Hand designs resides in the archives of the Massachusetts Institute of Technology.

Hand admired the *Coral* and hoped to build a schooner yacht along her lines one day, perhaps even use the design for another future project. Although Hand's wish about the schooner yacht never became a reality, he demonstrated his admiration by dedicating some time and expense to the project. He instructed one of his draftsmen, Walter A. Cross, to take the lines off the *Coral* (determine her "architectural specifications") and create offset drawings.

Three Hand vessels helped the town of Fairhaven celebrate its bicentennial in 2012. The *Guildive*, a motorsailer that is now in the charter business in Castine, Maine, visited in the spring. In early July, Arctic explorer Donald MacMillan's schooner *Bowdoin*, now the sail training vessel of Maine Maritime Academy, and the privately owned motor vessel *Tracker* welcomed visitors aboard and joined the parade of vessels that gathered at Butler Flats lighthouse.

Clifford Ashley

In a companion book to the mural *A Chart of the Whale Coast of New England c. 1810,* authors Seth Mendell and Connor Gaudet succinctly describe the work of Clifford W. Ashley, the mural's creator and a "neighbor" of Captain Tucker's:

> *Few people had both the practical knowledge of whaling and professional artistic training as Ashley, and he used these assets to produce works of literature and illustration that were respected and appreciated by old sea dogs and historians alike.*

The authors note that Ashley's book *The Yankee Whaler,* published in 1926, is "considered by many to be one of the most accurate and definitive portrayals of New England Whaling." His 1944 work, *The Ashley Book of Knots,* "is to this day renowned as the essential bible of knot tying with descriptions and illustrations of over 3,000 knots."

Ashley was also well known as a maritime artist, and he produced hundreds of nautical oil paintings. He was born in New Bedford in 1881, and in later years, he lived in Westport and maintained a studio in Fairhaven near the southwest corner of Washington and Water streets. His studio was located at the foot of Delano's Wharf. It was just a short walk to where the *Coral* tied up, and the artist often went aboard the schooner to gam with Captain Tucker whenever he wanted to take a break from his work.

George McDonald

In 1924, the natural elements forced Cap to replace both the mainmast and the foremast. They had both become weak from years of water gathering where the masts went through the deck. In an early example of recycling, or what was thought of at the time simply as "Yankee thrift," Cap obtained two masts that were salvaged from the *David K. Akin.* The *Akin* was a much larger schooner wrecked on Gooseberry Neck in Westport, the town just southeast of Fall River.

Cap enlisted the services of Frank C. Taylor, Inc., a marine construction company located on Middle Street not far from Cap's house, to deliver the masts to Delano's Wharf. Because the *Akin* was a large schooner and the *Coral*

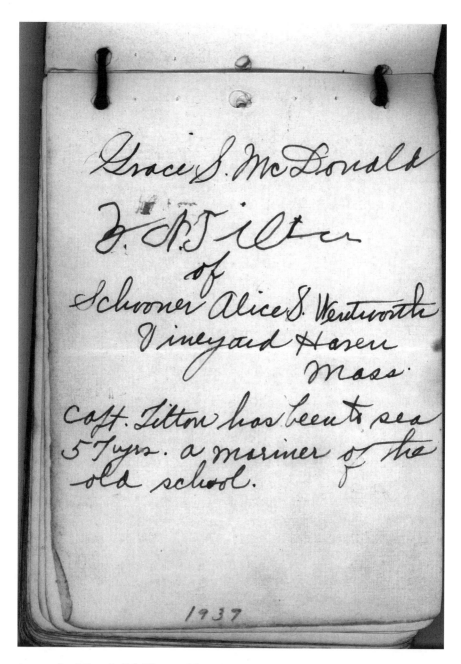

Autographs of Captain Zeb Tilton and Grace McDonald. 1939. *Courtesy of Robert Demanche.*

quite small, the *Akin*'s masts first needed customizing. This was a painstaking task but one that was ably done by the old ship's carpenter George McDonald of Water Street, whose shop sat near the wharf. McDonald spent many days cutting the masts down to size by hand. Not only did he need to cut each mast down to length, but he also had to round each one to the proper taper along its length. McDonald did this by first flattening the circumference to eight sides, then to sixteen, and so on. With the masts now the proper size, the rigging hardware was added. Taylor's crew then positioned the company's steam lighter, a type of workboat, between Delano's Wharf and the *Coral*, removed the old masts and installed the "new" ones.

Years later, McDonald's widow, Grace, married Captain Zeb Tilton in a wedding that drew national attention, the groom having by then attained folk legend status.

Ichabod Cromwell

The yawl boat was Captain Tucker's lifeline to the mainland whenever the *Coral* lay at anchor in a harbor. When he purchased the *Coral*, she only came with a small dinghy, but Ichabod Cromwell of 33 Water Street built Cap something more substantial after the Tuckers moved to that town. The yawl

The yawl boat. *Collection of Donald F. Tucker.*

boat had no engine, but at least Cap could now row to shore and back again or head over to a nearby schooner at anchor for a gam.

The yawl boat was a round-bottomed craft, no more than fifteen feet long, with a wine glass stern. When not in use, the yawl boat hung from the davits, a simple frame at the stern of the *Coral*. The yawl boat was so well designed and built that Cap felt it would have sailed extremely well. He always regretted not having built a centerboard into it for that purpose.

Cromwell was still active at age eighty-two, singlehandedly—but understandably very gradually—building a thirty-foot sloop in a lot next to his house.

CHAPTER 8

A Small Business

Unlike the larger companies whose huge schooners carried tremendous loads of coal, the *Coral* was for Captain Tucker a small business. To earn a living, he had to find and deliver cargoes on time and in good condition while ensuring the safety of his crew and himself. To do this required continual maintenance of the *Coral*. And as one would expect, he had to keep his costs down.

As owner and operator of the schooner, Captain Tucker wore many hats and needed to be skilled in many areas. He had to be a mariner, mechanic, carpenter, accountant and cook. He had to know the ins and outs of each port and know how to deal with customers and workers. He had to be enterprising enough to find the next cargo to carry.

Captain Tucker succeeded in all these areas. He was an honest person and very likeable. He had a reputation for being a square shooter and an all-around good man. He would never ask a crew member to do something that he would not do himself and would never put the vessel or the crew or himself in jeopardy. He treated his mates well, and he paid them well. Accordingly, turnover was low.

He loved sailing the *Coral*, and he loved the coasting business, difficult as it was. In later years, Cap took ownership of a gasoline filling station and garage. Although that line of work provided the family with much more income, Cap preferred the coasting trade and felt that the station and the garage were actually a nuisance.

The *Coral*, flying light with a bone in her teeth. Translation: The *Coral* sailing without a cargo, moving quickly through the water so as to create a prominent bow wave. *Collection of Donald F. Tucker.*

MAINTENANCE AND REPAIR

Captain Tucker had to keep the people who worked aboard the *Coral* safe and get the cargo to its destination on time and in good condition. He, therefore, had to maintain the *Coral* in good working order. Maintenance and repair were critical and were carried out in spring before sailing season, during the season as ongoing maintenance and in winter, when he prepared the *Coral* for about five months of inactivity during the cold weather. Cap saw to all this, and it was the single most important reason he never encountered trouble in all his years at sea.

With the arrival of March, and certainly no later than April, Cap would begin spring commissioning—getting the *Coral* ready for the coming work season. This involved mostly inspecting or testing the equipment and making any necessary repairs or replacements.

Cap would check the decking for rot, the anchor chain for rust and all lines and rigging for signs of wear. He would go up in the bosun's chair with a five-gallon pail of grease to grease the masts. The gaffs and booms

Ready to sail after spring commissioning. *Collection of Donald F. Tucker.*

would receive another coat of paint. The yawl boat and sails would come out of storage and the sails bent on. Cap would test the main engine, donkey engine and windlass to confirm that they all worked properly.

Periodically, the U.S. Coast Guard would also inspect the *Coral*. The inspector was an old sailor. He looked forward to traveling down to Fairhaven because he and Captain Tucker could gam and tell old stories by the wood stove and have a cup of coffee aboard the schooner. Meanwhile, a few recruits who traveled with the inspector did the actual inspection.

On one occasion, a young recruit wrote up Cap for not having a steam line going into the paint locker. This storage space for flammable substances, such as paint thinner and turpentine, was located below deck at the bow of the vessel. Regulations dictated that commercial vessels run a steam line to the paint locker so that if a fire should break out, you could turn the steam line on to put out the fire.

The recruit reasoned that the *Coral* was a commercial vessel that had a paint locker; therefore, she needed a steam line. This gave the old inspector and Cap quite a laugh for some time. The *Coral* was powered by the wind and gasoline, not steam, and so there was no steam generator and therefore no steam line running to the paint locker. There was never even a hint of steam anywhere aboard the schooner, except when Captain Tucker happened to make hot soup on a cold day or when things didn't go well.

Maintenance and repair during the warmer months was ongoing. When necessary, Cap had the *Coral* hauled out at a shipyard when the hull required cleaning, painting or inspecting. In the Newport years, this meant a one-day stop in Greenport while waiting for a charter. Cost for hauling the vessel and painting the bottom: ten dollars. When the *Coral* was based in Fairhaven, Captain Tucker hauled her out at Kelley's boatyard to clean the bottom and to make repairs.

Whoever shipped as mate usually took care of maintenance and repair above the waterline. Cap's older sons, who sailed aboard the *Coral* during the 1930s, were not exempt from these tasks. They may have known the boss, but that didn't mean that they could get away with doing a sub-par job.

In his *Log of the "Coral,"* crewman George Gale recorded some of the work he did when he first came aboard. His entries provide some interesting insights into day-to-day maintenance and repairs aboard the schooner:

July 10, 1923
Painted out the after bunk & the locker & caulked the centerboard trunk where it had been sweating.

Claude Tucker Jr. (left), Captain Tucker and Donald Tucker aboard the *Coral* on the north side of Taylor's marine construction company yard. 1940. *Photograph by Helen Tucker Davidson; Collection of Donald F. Tucker.*

July 14, 1923
    We strapped the cat fall on the port anchor, hove it on the dock, & chipped and red-leaded the anchor & a couple fathom of chain.

July 18, 1923
    The skipper painted the masthead today and I painted the black bulwarks and name, bow & transom.

July 19, 1923
    Tarred down the masthead eyes, and red-leaded the face shrouds. Another dirty job done. Painted the white on boom & gaff jaws & ends. I chipped & red-leaded the iron-work of the windlass.

August 3, 1923
    Patched the stern of the skiff & painted the inside this afternoon.

Gale also recorded some difficulties, both mechanical and physical, that he and Cap had on a trip from Fairhaven to Nantucket to Mattapoisett in 1925:

Sunday, June 14, Fairhaven
Just got our headline on dock 7:30 at Washington St. & the damn engine went blooey. No savvy why…Started overhauling the engine found timing gears on camshaft are stripped…Putting in new set of camshaft gears…dirty damn job.

Saturday, June 20, Nantucket
Started discharging 7:30 finished 8:30. Cut out forward cylinder of Engine—running on three.

Then later
Through the hole [Woods Hole] *4:30. Hell of a time getting through. Engine all in.*

Monday, June 22, Mattapoisett
Started to put on a new forward cylinder & the damn thing won't fit. Skipper wrenched his back lifting the cylinder. So did I. She doesn't fit—sent it back to the shop. Got a mechanic after dinner, set the engine up & got her going.

It probably didn't require much artistic talent to touch up the schooner's name and port of enrollment painted on the stern, but the task fell to George Gale, who likely regarded it simply as a job that had to be done. Although Captain Tucker and the *Coral* had moved to Fairhaven, Cap did not change the port of enrollment from Newport. He reasoned that it wasn't a critical issue, and there was no taxation at the time. His decision had more to do with avoiding unnecessary bureaucracy than anything else.

When Cap and the *Coral* were based in Newport, the *Coral* sailed year round, except for when there was a likelihood that the destination port was iced in. When they were based in Fairhaven in the 1930s, Nantucket counted for much of Cap's work. Because little went on there in the colder months, he would lay the *Coral* up at Delano's Wharf beginning around late November.

Cap wasn't concerned about ice forming around the *Coral* during these colder months in Fairhaven, since it wouldn't freeze hard enough to cause any structural damage to the hull. He could not just leave the *Coral* at the wharf as is, however. The sails required thorough drying and storing. Likewise, the yawl boat was stored upside down under canvas in the family yard. The windlass and the donkey engine were covered with canvas. The

The *Coral*, laid up for the winter at Delano's Wharf in ice-covered New Bedford Harbor. *Collection of Donald F. Tucker.*

main engine needed winterizing. The bilge pump had to be rebuilt. Hatches needed battening down, and the water keg needed emptying. It was all very cold but essential work.

Food

Captain Tucker, like most others in the coasting trade, worked day and night, and it was common for him to go for days without a leisurely, carefully planned meal. Such a meal only came while waiting in port. When this occurred, Cap prepared meals in the main cabin on the sole source of heat: a small wood-burning stove. Cap was an excellent cook and, unlike some schooner operators, did not skimp on food. He always had the coffee pot going.

Cap often struck up a friendship with crew of lobster and fishing boats that lay alongside. On these occasions, fresh seafood was the treat that evening. If no fishing boats were to be seen, Captain Tucker broke out a box of salt cod and made a creamed cod dish served on mashed potatoes.

Captain Tucker always had a fair amount of canned goods and dried and cooked cereals on hand. He kept the *Coral* well stocked with corned beef and dried beef for creamed beef on toast. All sorts of beans—navy pea, kidney and yellow-eyed—went into the large crock of salt pork and molasses that always seemed to be on the stove.

To prevent waste, Cap selected only the bare minimum of perishable food, such as fresh fruit and vegetables. He equipped the *Coral* with an icebox, though ice was an expensive commodity and not always available. Fresh water was stored in a wooden barrel on deck on the starboard side near the wheel.

Canned evaporated milk replaced fresh milk aboard the *Coral*. Evidently, if you got used to it, it was fine. Captain Tucker's son Donald certainly never did, and the young mate automatically gave any meal served with evaporated milk only one star.

Captain Tucker's delicious johnnycakes were a favorite. The same big bowl of batter appeared in the preparation of just about every meal. He also made sourdough bread and biscuits.

For dessert, Cap made a great apple pie, as well as a variation of this American favorite. This was apple slump, which was simply apple chunks baked in dough. Other commons desserts were "barge pie," which was molasses on bread and butter, and another variation, applesauce on bread and butter.

Sometimes the task of preparing meals fell to crewman George Gale, who wrote this in his *Log of the "Coral"*:

> *O, I am the cook & the messman too*
> *And the mate of the Coral schooner*
> *The bos'n tight & the midship mite*
> *And the bacon & spud harpooner.*

The *Coral*, passing the *Cross Rip* lightship. Note the light atop each mast. Circa 1923.
Collection of Donald F. Tucker.

Cap and his mate could relate to some extent to crew members aboard lightships, such as the *Cross Rip*, who spent weeks at a time cooped up with each other aboard a vessel whose main purpose was to warn other vessels to keep away. Because many of the crew members aboard the *Cross Rip* lived in New Bedford, they no doubt looked forward to the city newspaper thrown to them as the *Coral* sailed by.

Time Away from the Office

Whenever the *Coral* was tied up at home in Fairhaven, Captain Tucker and his family enjoyed many happy activities together. The family kept a beautiful garden that was a combination of the practical and the aesthetic—mostly vegetables with a sprinkling of flowers at the insistence of Cap's wife, Catherine. Over the years, the barking and companionship of several pet dogs—coon hounds, bird dogs, rabbit hounds and just plain mutts—livened the Tucker household.

Captain Tucker once again took up beekeeping, primarily as a hobby. He and his sons constructed the hives from nail kegs, set them in the woods and retrieved them for the honey in the fall. They spent cold days ice fishing in nearby lakes and streams and many fall evenings frost fishing with a spear and kerosene lantern on the beach in Fairhaven. They looked forward to early morning duck hunting, with a thermos of hot chocolate to share in the duck blind. At other times, they would gather grapes and elderberries for making wine.

These relaxing activities offered a chance to forget bad weather, difficult cargoes, repairs and other inherent problems of running a schooner. Though it certainly was a tough life, it was a good life for all of the family. Captain Tucker would not have traded his experiences for the world.

CHAPTER 9

Scenes from the Twenties

C aptain Tucker's travels didn't carry him to exotic locales, but that didn't stop life from being interesting. Here are some of the schooner captains, mates, friends, acquaintances and even the occasional unexpected visitor that might cross his path on any given day.

George Gale

George Gale knew that a coasting schooner could not make money tied to the dock, and like other coastermen, he grew restless when a departure was delayed. A five-day wait due to bad weather prompted him to write this in his journal: "I'm sick of hanging onto our shore lines...guess I might as well become a citizen of Fairhaven now." Unfortunately, he had to cool his heels for another three days before shoving off.

Gale was a man of many talents and abilities. He was a sailor, artist, collector of whaling artifacts, boatbuilder and musician. He served as mate aboard the *Coral* over the course of three years in the mid-1920s, and he drew from his extensive maritime experience, his natural abilities and his art education to create highly regarded etchings and watercolors. Maritime museums and discerning individuals collect his works to this day.

Gale was born in 1893 in Bristol, Rhode Island, and grew up on the waterfront there. As a child he attended Saturday morning class at the Rhode

George Gale at the helm of the *Coral*, hauling cordwood from Assonet to Nantucket. The cordwood is piled on the quarterdeck as high as possible for the helmsman to still see over and for it to not interfere with the boom. Circa 1923. *Collection of Donald F. Tucker.*

Island School of Design. He left high school after a year and shipped out on a freighter out of New York. He eventually served on various coastal vessels.

He served as chief quartermaster of a Luckenbach steamer in the merchant marine in World War I and survived a torpedo from a German under-sea boat that was not aware that the Armistice had been signed two days earlier.

Following World War I, Gale won a scholarship and returned to the Rhode Island School of Design, where he learned the fundamentals of etching. He took an immediate liking to the medium and built his own etching press, using the cast-iron wheel of a schooner and discarded oak ships' timbers.

Gale created meticulously accurate portrayals of maritime scenes. "But, while [art school] helped me," he said in an interview, "I guess the real reason is because I've worked hard all my life and know what it is to feel my muscles ache."

Gale was already familiar with schooners and the oyster trade when he approached Captain Tucker about working aboard the *Coral*. He lived in

Catting the Anchor. Etching of Captain Tucker and the *Coral* by George Gale. *Collection of Donald F. Tucker*.

Barrington, Rhode Island, and whenever he had to report to the *Coral*, he took a train to Fall River and then a trolley to Fairhaven or Mattapoisett. He often took a turn at the helm, and he was a natural at maintenance and mechanics. He even contributed by taking photographs.

Gale's works often featured the *Coral*. In his etching *Catting the Anchor*, he portrays the method used to secure the anchor to the schooner so it would not bounce back and forth while underway. Captain Tucker is lassoing one of the anchor's flukes with the aid of block and tackle. The windlass has by this time hoisted the anchor chain through the hawse pipe, which is not pictured but is forward of the anchor. The master link at the top of the anchor is fastened by a small chain to the "cat," which is the wooden piece above the rail.

Gale collected whaling memorabilia, and when in New Bedford with the *Coral*, he took the opportunity to study and portray relics of the whaling industry such as the *Charles W. Morgan, Wanderer, John R. Manta* and *Athlete*. Observing the final years of that era, he wrote in his *Log* on July 13, 1923,

"The whaling schooner William A. Graber is tied up on the other side of the S.O. wharf, full of oil & can't sell it."

Two days later, he added these two entries: "The schooner Claudia is stow down, as the owners can get only four bits a gallon for sperm oil, so are holding it for a better market later on…painted a watercolor of the Claudia & Romance, a whaler and an ex-packet."

Chanteys, those work songs so important aboard ships, were not part of the coastal schooner story, but music in general seemed to find a home whenever the *Coral* was in port and Gale was aboard as mate. Gale would sit on the deck and play his guitar, sometimes for his own enjoyment, sometimes to entertain people on the dock who would stop to listen. Often, Cap would get his harmonica out and hold court with Gale. On one such occasion, Gale met a woman in the audience named Mary, whom he would eventually marry.

Another time he took his show on the road:

> *Sunday, August 5, 1923*
> *Kelly came in after me in the yawl & we went aboard the Nantisco & played for the Old man and his wife.*

In his *Log*, Gale left a glimpse of his musical interests by including chord diagrams for a four-stringed instrument and words to songs such as *Sweet Hawaiian Girl of Mine, Black Ball Line, Pierre le Grand, Juan Fernandez, Walking the Plank, Tortuga, Sharks, The Calabazo* and *Buccaneers*.

Gale's stay aboard the *Coral* came to an abrupt end in Mattapoisett on August 25, 1925, when he worked until 3:00 p.m., "had a row with the skipper" and was paid off. His *Log of the "Coral"* gives little clue as to the nature of their argument, except for the entry, "Now the whole damn family is coming aboard." Captain Tucker and Gale later renewed their friendship.

Following the *Coral*, Gale found work for about the next four years as quartermaster of the ferryboat *Bristol* and later as drawbridge tender on the Washington Bridge in Providence. These jobs kept him close to the water while allowing him time to work at his art.

Gale also built sailing vessels. His first was *Hurricane*, a sloop he built for his father for ten dollars and later sold to friend George Keyes who renamed her *Spray*. Using material salvaged from *Stormalong*, a vessel George Gale built previously, he built *Sharpshooter*, a two-master schooner, about 1940.

Gale later created illustrations for the Providence *Journal*, as well as the chapter heading illustrations for the newspaper's book *The History of Yachting on Narragansett Bay: 1922–1945* by Arthur "Jeff" Davis.

Exhibitions of Gale's work included a show at the Mariners Club at the Peirce and Kilburn shipyard. The show featured thirty-four etchings, all scenes of whaleships and whaling, except for two etchings of the *Coral—Lee Bowing the Tide* and *Decks To.* Fairhaven photographer Albert Cook Church noted in a newspaper review: "The various prints depicting the harpooning of a sperm whale bristle with vigor and action, while the entire series show strong originality and a thorough knowledge of all the various phases of whaling and fitting out."

A newspaper article described a 1963 show at the Bristol Art Museum in Rhode Island:

> *His prints of ships, men at work on the docks or at whaling, and the big draft horses used in the wharf areas are things of unimaginable truth and beauty of line: virile, active, arresting.*
>
> *Strong in color value, they are anatomically perfect and the technique shows the free and easy style of a craftsman as thoroughly familiar with the eccentricities of acid and needle as he was with his subject.*

Gale's *Log* lists what appear to be names of places and institutions to which he sent prints of his works for possible exhibition, loan or sale:

> *William H. Vanderbilt, 815 Fifth Avenue, New York*
> *Society of Printmakers of California,*
> *c/o Los Angeles Museum of History, Science and Art*
> *Yachting, 25 West 43 Street, New York*
> *National Arts Club, Grammercy Park, New York*
> *Tilden-Thurber Galleries*
> *Country Life*
> *Kennedy's, New York*
> *Other individuals*

Institutions holding his works include the Metropolitan Museum of Art, New York; Old Dartmouth Historical Society, New Bedford; Nantucket Historical Association; Mystic Seaport Museum; and Bishop Museum, Honolulu, Hawaii.

Captain Tucker and George Gale last saw each other at an exhibit of Gale's artwork in Barrington in the late 1940s. He passed away in Barrington in 1951.

THE WANDERER

The bark *Wanderer* was the last square-rigged whaleship to sail out of New Bedford. She was built in Mattapoisett in 1878, the same year as the *Coral*. The *Wanderer* departed the famous whaling port on August 25, 1924, and

The *Wanderer* drying sails at New Bedford. *Photograph by Steve Crowley; Collection of Donald F. Tucker.*

went aground on the rocks off the island of Cuttyhunk in a hurricane the next day.

On the first night, the *Wanderer* anchored off Mishaum Point in Dartmouth, not far to the west. Fierce hurricane winds pushed the whaleship across Buzzards Bay toward Penikese and Cuttyhunk. Foreseeing disaster, the crew abandoned the vessel in two whaleboats, eight men to a boat. One whaleboat safely reached Cuttyhunk. The other was rescued by the *Sow and Pigs* lightship. The *Wanderer* herself ended up on the rocks off Sow and Pigs Reef along the island's southwest end the next day.

When the storm subsided, valuable items from the ship, such as the captain's chest and chronometers, were sent ashore to Cuttyhunk. A reporter called the shoreline a "dismal scene…littered with wreckage and the contents of seamen's chests, spread out upon the grass to dry out in the sun."

The *Wanderer* had been outfitted with sails by the C.E. Beckman Company, a sailmaker and ship's chandler in New Bedford. Beckman's hired Cap and the *Coral* to recover the sails. Instead of trying to maneuver the *Coral* alongside the vessel on the rocks, however, Cap waited until they too were on the Cuttyhunk shore.

Happily, the cat, found in the ship's cabin, also made it off the ship safely. The feline (possibly frightened, but who knows) came by way of the breeches buoy, a rescue device used to remove people from wrecked vessels, and was adopted by the owners of the Wood Mansion on the island.

Captain Irving D. Talbot

After he sold the *Coral* to Captain Tucker, Captain Talbot bought the *George F. Carman*, a schooner built in Patchogue, New York, on Long Island. He had an engine installed in the *Carman* at Reed Brothers, later known as Crowninshield's, his cousin's shipyard in Somerset. Throughout the years, Captain Talbot and Captain Tucker often sailed to the same destination "in company," that is, in sight of each other.

Bill Talbot recalled carrying oysters, coal, lumber, sand, clay and other cargoes with his father aboard the *Carman*:

> *We carried Long Island potatoes from Mattatuck Creek—that was the backside of Long Island—to Providence and New Bedford. The First National or A&P would take a load. Or if they didn't take the load, we'd*

*take a chance and buy the load, and my father'd go ashore in Newport, call
up a dozen people, and he'd sell the load to somebody.*

Once in a while, the cargo would be ice: "There'd be a breakdown of
an ice plant somewhere, such as Nantucket. They'd bring the ice down by
[railroad] car to Woods Hole, and we'd run a few loads from there."

CAPTAIN EMIL JOHNSON

On April 10, 1926, Captain Tucker sailed the *Coral* in company with Captain
Talbot in the *George F. Carman* and Captain Emil Johnson of South Swansea in
the *David K. Akin*. Captain Johnson owned two other coasters, the *Stephen Taber*
and the *Falcon*. Tucker, Talbot and Johnson were all headed to Cape Cod with
oysters. As they proceeded on their journey that day, they ducked into Newport
and anchored due to bad weather. The next morning, Captain Johnson decided
he would get under way, even though the weather was still nasty.

The captain always wore a long overcoat, and this morning was no
exception. He went forward to start his donkey engine to weigh anchor.
Unfortunately, he caught his coat in the winch, and according to a newspaper
report, "he was whirled off his feet, his head striking against the pump."

Captain Johnson's hired hand did not know how to shut the engine down,
so all he could do was shout. When Captain Talbot and Captain Tucker
heard the commotion, they jumped into their yawl boats and rowed over
to the *Akin*. Climbing aboard, they shut the engine down, but they were not
in time. They transported Captain Johnson to Newport Hospital where he
soon died.

BEN WATERWORTH

Another longtime mate and lifelong friend was Ben Waterworth. Waterworth
was a deepwater sailor and a good storyteller to boot. He turned to working
aboard yachts and was between jobs when Cap brought him on to work. He
sailed as mate in the late 1920s and early '30s.

After a few seasons on the *Coral*, Waterworth left to run a small schooner
that he bought, the *Herman L. Rogers*. Waterworth owned the *Rogers* only

The *Herman L. Rogers* aground in Wareham. She was previously owned by Ben Waterworth. *Collection of Donald F. Tucker.*

briefly. He sold her to new owners who planned to pick up a load of watermelon in Georgia and haul it to Boston. The new owners took the *Rogers* out for a trial run before heading south, but it was an exceedingly hard sail in Buzzards Bay, and the schooner started taking on water. They then beached the *Rogers* in Wareham, possibly on Great Neck, where she eventually went to pieces.

Waterworth turned to serving as captain aboard yachts. During his time aboard the *Coral*, he grew to love Buzzards Bay and the near coast, so if the yacht owner had no preferred destination, he would stay local. For years, Waterworth was a fixture around Kelley's boatyard in Fairhaven. He owned a beautiful little friendship sloop, the *Banshee*, which he moored not far from Delano's Wharf. Donald Tucker's catboat later survived Hurricane Gloria on Waterworth's old mooring.

When Waterworth's health suffered in later life, he went to live at Sailors' Snug Harbor, a home for retired seafarers in Duxbury. Sailors' Snug Harbor was located in the former Powder Point School, a large, three-story building built in 1913 that faced the bay. The building had

Ben Waterworth and his friendship sloop, the *Banshee*, at Kelley's boatyard. Early 1960s. *Collection of Donald F. Tucker.*

also served as a summer hotel and was the home of the National Sailors Home from about 1931 to 1957 when Sailors' Snug Harbor bought the property. The number of men at Sailors' Snug Harbor dwindled as time went on. When Waterworth lived there, he was one of only four men on the property. Eventually, several local residents bought the premises, and the building succumbed to the wrecking ball in 1974. Waterworth eventually passed away in a nursing home in Plymouth.

CAPTAIN TUCKER WAS READY TO TAKE A CHARTER whenever and wherever he could find one. Sometimes he would go ashore to call his regular customers in the oyster trade or on Nantucket. Other times, he might pick up work just by being in the right place at the right time.

Many years later, Cap recalled a time when he and Ben Waterworth were in Greenport, desperate to find a charter. At last they were hired to deliver a load of brick, and the seller gave Cap a charter party describing the conditions of the delivery. Now, it's one thing if you don't read the fine print, but it can definitely get you into a jam if you don't read the regular print. Here's how Cap told the story:

This year I went over there [to Greenport], *and there wasn't an oyster movin'. Schooners were just layin' there. I couldn't get a load nowhere. After a couple of days, a fella comes down out of Peconic Bay from a brickyard. He said he had twenty-five thousand brick to go to the east end of Fishers Island and wanted to know if I'd take 'em.*

So, I gave him a good price, and he took me up on it. You oughta see them bricks fly. I never saw anything like it. I was on my way before noontime with twenty-five thousand of brick, all on the deck. They'd pick up four or five or six brick, side by side, and they'd take and toss 'em to the next guy. And he'd grab them. They were still right together. I never saw anything like it.

Well, we got right under way. They had given me a charter party. I shoved it in my pocket, never looked at it. On the way down, I happened to feel it in my pocket and took it out and looked at it. It said that they had three days to unload me. That didn't sit very good with me. I didn't want to lose that much time just waiting around for them to unload.

So, after a while, the boss come down and I met him on the dock. The first thing he says was, "Have you got a charter party?"

I couldn't tell him "no" very well. So, I said, "Yes."

He said, "Let me see it."

He read where he had three days to unload. "Oh," he says, "that's just right for me. I've got plenty of help, but they're all busy. I'll need that three days."

Well, I did a lot of thinkin'. I said, "If you want those bricks, the best thing you can do is get a gang here and get 'em off my deck fast. Otherwise, you'll be pickin' 'em up off the bottom."

He said, "What's the matter?"

I said, "I sprung a bad leak comin' down here, and I got to get to the shipyard," even though the vessel wasn't really leakin'.

He says, "Can you keep 'em afloat tonight?"

"Well," I says, "yes, with my boy pumpin' steady all night."

Early the next mornin', I saw the boss comin'. I put Ben to work with the pump. There wasn't any water comin' out, but he couldn't see that because of all the brick piled up. I sized the boss up. I figured he didn't know much about vessels.

He says, "Gee, kept her afloat, eh?"

I said, "By God, that was some tough night, I'll tell ya'. There was pumps all night long pumpin'. We could just keep her clear."

He said, "I'll have the gang right down here." And believe me, they could handle brick. I was all unloaded before noon. They took 'em off faster than they put 'em on.

Then, I was afraid that he'd come aboard and see the deck all dry, so I met him up on the dock. He handed me a check. I looked at it, and I saw it was all right.

But by that time, the weather had gotten dirty—rainin' and blowin'. Awful day. And it happened that the wind was blowin' right off the dock. So, I ran down and jumped aboard and I hollered, "Let go of those lines!" Inside of a minute, the wind took us right away from the dock where nobody could get aboard.

I didn't know whether to go north, south, east or west. I didn't know where to go. She headed away on the port tack. That had us headin' west. So, I let her go.

In the later years, when Captain Tucker visited Waterworth or other old friends, the talk always turned to schooner life. Cap recalled a story Waterworth told about the time he was on a ship that was in port south of the equator. Waterworth liked it down there, and he thought he'd like to relocate for awhile.

Apparently, Waterworth had ventured away from the port area when he made his decision to desert. A railroad track ran nearby, and he figured that if he walked the track far enough, he'd come across a village. For two days, he walked and walked and walked. He was dying of thirst when he finally reached a little town. As Waterworth passed the drinking establishment, a man standing outside the door sang out, "How'd you like a beer?" Still dying of thirst, Waterworth said, "I'd love it." Waterworth sits down inside with the man, who buys him two or three beers, and then the man exclaims, "Well, 'bout time we's gettin' back aboard the ship, isn't it!" Waterworth's host was one of the men stationed around the area to catch deserters. He probably made fifty bucks for bringing Waterworth back aboard the ship.

In another story, Waterworth briefly "joined" the Australian Army while working aboard a square-rigger. He was in Fremantle, Australia, at the time. One of the ways the country got men for the army was simple but effective. Women would ride around the pubs on horseback, leading another saddled horse, and they'd holler, "Fill the empty saddle!" Waterworth had been ashore at a pub there, drinking with his crewmates. Finally, they decided to return to the ship, and just as they went out onto the street, a gang of women comes by singing, "Fill the empty saddle!" Waterworth and his mates all climbed aboard the horses, only to wake up the next morning in the army barracks along with all the non–crew members the women had collected the day and night before.

One of Waterworth's crewmates in the barracks was a man who, Waterworth thought, was no sailor but could make more trouble than all the rest of the crew put together. By and by, both the captain of the ship and an army officer came into the barracks and looked the crowd over.

"There's one of my crew," the skipper would say and call him out.

Eventually, the captain called out Waterworth. But when the captain and the army officer passed the troublemaker, the skipper didn't look at him, and they kept walking.

"Here I am, Captain!" the troublesome crew member hollered out.

The army officer asked, "You know that man?"

"Never saw him before in my life."

When the captain had collected his crewmen, minus one, they went back aboard the ship and loaded for Capetown, South Africa. After delivering the cargo to Capetown, they took on another load and sailed back to Fremantle. As they were unloading there, who but the troublemaker comes aboard for a visit, wearing his army uniform. It seemed that he was welcomed by at least some of the crew because they decided to go ashore after supper, and they invited him along.

"No," the troublemaker said, "I think I'll spend a while in my old home here."

Thinking nothing of it, his buddies went ashore and spent the evening, leaving him alone in the fo'c'sle. When they returned, he was gone. Again, thinking nothing of it, they eventually loaded for New York and set sail.

The weather turned cold for the captain and crew as the ship's course took them into the lower latitudes of the Roaring Forties. Accordingly, Waterworth went down to his sea bag to get warmer clothes. Reaching to the bottom of it to get some heavier clothes, he instead hauled up the troublemaker's army uniform. Waterworth had no choice but to continue the voyage dressed as a soldier. Meanwhile, the troublemaker had escaped from the army wearing Waterworth's clothes.

CAPTAIN ZEB TILTON

Zebulon Northrop Tilton of Martha's Vineyard was a friend of Captain Tucker and his family. Zeb owned the *Alice S. Wentworth*, a coasting schooner that continued to carry cargo with him as captain until about 1942. The *Alice S. Wentworth* was the last working coaster based in the area from Cape Cod to Narragansett Bay and perhaps even farther on either side.

Zeb was a celebrated schooner man in his day. He appeared on national radio shows and was a friend of luminaries such as actor Jimmy Cagney and others on the Vineyard. Zeb was known for his strength, wit, charm with the ladies, nautical abilities and appetite.

Zeb and the *Wentworth* frequently dropped anchor in Fairhaven and would always stop at the Tucker household for a visit and a meal. Captain Tucker's young son Donald, always in awe of Zeb's size, was equally in awe of the visitor's enormous appetite. Mrs. Tucker took Zeb's eating as a personal compliment to her cooking.

One evening Zeb came to dinner, and Mrs. Tucker laid out a feast. Zeb just kept on eating. The family thought he would burst. Finally, he pushed his plate away, and Captain Tucker asked if he cared for dessert.

"Sure, Cap. Meal isn't over 'til dessert is stowed."

So, Mrs. Tucker cut Zeb at least a quarter of one of the deep-dish apple pies she had made and offered him cream cheese for a topping. At that time, cream cheese came in a three-pound block wrapped in foil in a wooden box. She placed the block on a plate and set it before Zeb. Thinking it was ice cream, he lopped off at least half of the block of cream cheese for his pie and proceeded to stow his dessert.

Captain Tucker's daughter Kathleen was Zeb's favorite, and the young child's light complexion and blonde hair prompted him to nickname her Whitey. She could not recognize the difference between schooners, so if the spars of the *Wentworth* came into view while the *Coral* was away, Kathleen would expect her father to show up for dinner.

CHARLIE SAYLE

Another renowned mariner in his own right was Charlie Sayle. By the time Sayle moved to Nantucket at about age twenty-one, he had already worked on the Great Lakes, sailed to the British Isles on a merchant vessel and shipped on a Gloucester fishing schooner.

Sayle also sailed on coasting vessels, including the *Alice S. Wentworth* on which he made about twelve to fourteen trips per year during the 1930s. When Captain Tucker was in Nantucket, Sayle would often come down to the dock to meet him and invite him to the house for dinner and hours of conversation about schooner life.

BILL McCOY

The Eighteenth Amendment to the United States Constitution prohibited the manufacture, sale and distribution of alcoholic beverages. Congress subsequently passed the Volstead Act, which provided funds for the amendment's enforcement. One of the most well-known targets of this enforcement was rumrunner Bill McCoy. His large and fast schooner *Arethusa* was known to lay off the northeastern coast of the U.S. just outside the territorial limit of enforcement.

The Prohibition Era lasted from 1920 until 1933. While some rumrunners sold alcohol of questionable quality and content, sometimes even causing serious illness to the consumer, McCoy touted his product as the safest and finest.

Fast schooners running silently in the darkness of night made excellent vehicles for transporting cases of the alcohol from supply boats offshore to any of the secret drop-off points along the jagged New England coastline. Although rumrunning was a risky undertaking, many people made their fortunes spiriting the contraband cargo into the mainland. Captain Tucker consistently turned his back on these operations, although his reputation as an experienced, reliable businessman would certainly have raised him above suspicion. Had the *Coral* been a faster schooner, perhaps he might have done it.

Once when the *Arethusa* lay off the coast south of Newport, McCoy's men aboard the schooner were unable to get their load ashore to Providence and began to get anxious. McCoy approached Captain Tucker and asked if he was interested in delivering the cargo. His offer included placing enough money in escrow to pay any fines Cap might incur if he got caught, to bribe a judge and jury or even buy the *Coral* back at auction if the government seized her. Captain Tucker refused to take McCoy's offer, and many thought him crazy to have rejected the idea. The *Arethusa* eventually returned to Canada after McCoy apparently found some owners of small, fast powerboats to off-load her.

The *Coral* encountered other rumrunners from time to time as well, and George Gale wrote this in his *Log*:

Sailing down through Vineyard Sound
On a dark & blustery night
The darken'd rum fleet looms ahead
Hove to—without a light.
"Hard up the helm!" the lookout yells
"Schooner dead ahead!"
The sleepy helmsman growls "Hell's bells!"
"Some damn fool leather head!"
But he whirls the spokes—her head pays off
She smokes by the rum ship's lee
The helmsman yawns "A helluva life
Got any tobacker?" says he.
So the coaster barges along
To the forefoot's husky snore;
As long as coasters live & swim
Who the hell wants to work ashore?

Gale also made this entry for Wednesday, July 29, 1925: "I went over to Kelley's wharf and painted the name and port of hail on the rumrunner, Roenomore. Tainted money I was paid—'Taint theirs any more."

Bill Talbot remembers that his father, Captain Irving D. Talbot, ran into a similar situation:

We were offered two loads of rum for $9,000. My father said, "No, I don't want to die with that on my conscience." So, a guy [we knew] took the contract, and it went to his head. He had two other men runnin' the boat. He went down to get aboard one night, and they found him the next mornin' with a death grip on the piling when the tide went down. He was drunk and tried to board the boat but could not manage it.

CHAPTER 10

The Great Depression

The Great Depression was a long and severe economic downturn in the United States and other nations. In the United States, it began after the stock market crash in October 1929. Millions of people lost their jobs, and many had no choice but to rely on the government or charitable organizations for food. Industrial production for World War II at the end of the 1930s finally lifted economic conditions in our nation.

For schooners in the coasting trade, there was less cargo to carry due to both the economy and the competition from railroads, steam tug-and-barges, steam colliers and trucks. Fortunately, Captain Tucker had the gas station and garage to provide the majority of the family income, and he continued to get some charters, mostly for gasoline. Family members helped out at both the garage and aboard the *Coral*, which helped lower the costs of running these businesses.

PARK GARAGE

In the late 1920s, a friend took out a mortgage from Captain Tucker to help buy an Esso gas station, auto repair garage and house situated between Main and Middle Streets. This was the Park Garage, later the site of Park Motors. Unfortunately, the business suffered due to the stock market crash in 1929, and Captain Tucker was obliged to take over the buildings and property to

The *Coral* at Fish Island, New Bedford. The New Bedford–Fairhaven Bridge is above and to the right in the photo. 1920s. *Collection of Donald F. Tucker.*

protect his investment. In 1929, the family took up residence in the house at 84 Main Street, part of the Park Garage property. Donald Tucker was born there in 1932. The house no longer stands.

Because Captain Tucker and his oldest son, Bill, were often away on the *Coral*, the rest of the family pitched in at the garage. Helen, the second child, established herself as a success in the workplace. Dressed in Esso coveralls, she pumped gas, repaired flat tires and changed oil each day until younger brother Frank came home from school and took over her duties. Helen was an intelligent girl as well as a hard worker, and she kept up with her classmates academically by obtaining homework assignments from the teachers.

Captain Tucker especially enjoyed having his sons sail with him when they were old enough to work and out of school. The boys picked up where Ben Waterworth left off after his tenure on the *Coral*. Being aboard was good experience for the boys, and they in turn provided some welcome family labor in the midst of the Depression. While son Bill attended Fairhaven High School, he was released early in the spring to help outfit the schooner and then sail aboard it all summer. Sons Frank and Claude Jr. followed right along as they grew older. Donald sailed many times on the *Coral* until the age of six.

The boys were thrilled to have their own place to sleep up forward in the fo'c'sle. A small forward hatch led down to their bunks below deck. Captain Tucker called it the "booby hatch," referring to his sons as "boobies in the booby hatch." The boys didn't know that the booby is a tropical bird so named by sailors because of its extraordinary stupidity. Even if they had known, they probably wouldn't have cared. In their minds, sleeping up in the fo'c'sle like the sailors of old was a sure sign that they were grownups.

All four sons eventually went on to serve their country as members of the armed forces. Schooner experience coupled with training from their father prepared Captain Tucker's three oldest sons to become good navy men. Bill and Frank served in World War II and Claude Jr. during the Korean War. Donald chose to serve in the air force during the Korean War.

THE DONKEY ENGINE

In 1931, Captain Tucker installed a donkey engine, a one-cylinder diesel engine that helped raise sails and hoist cargo. With little money to pay a mate in those early Depression days and his children attending school for a good part of the year, Cap had to sail solo on occasion. The main reason for the engine, however, was that he was awarded a contract that required more power for hoisting than men could muster.

The contract was a lucrative one, and it paid for the engine quickly. It called for Cap to haul creosote timbers from New Bedford to Vineyard

The *Coral* in Nantucket. Captain Tucker runs the windlass hoisting barrels of paving oil.
The donkey engine is located aft of the foremast, the winch forward of the foremast. 1935.
Collection of Donald F. Tucker.

Haven. From there, the timbers were trucked to Oak Bluffs and used to
construct a bulkhead, the first retaining wall built along the town waterfront.
For six months, six days a week, in any type of weather, the routine was the
same: the timbers were loaded, Cap sailed for the Vineyard, the timbers
were unloaded and he sailed back.

Captain Tucker purchased the engine from the Hathaway Machinery
Company, then located on Elm Street in New Bedford. (The company later
moved to Fairhaven.) He mounted the donkey engine on deck, just aft of the
foremast. A cable attached to the timber ran up to the gaff and down again
to a winch, passing through a series of blocks-and-tackles along the way. The
donkey engine turned the winch, which pulled the cable coming down from
the gaff. It was a sequence of events that occurred innumerable times during
that six-month period.

THE LEG O' MUTTON SAIL

As time went on in the 1930s, the *Coral's* mainsail began to show signs of
rot and normal wear-and-tear at an upper corner. The damage was to be

The *Coral* bound out of Nantucket with the leg o' mutton mainsail. Mid-1930s. *Collection of Donald F. Tucker.*

expected as it was the same mainsail in use when Captain Tucker purchased the schooner in 1915. Typically, the repairs called for having a new sail made, but as money was tight, Cap was open to alternatives.

A good friend of his named John Durant was a longtime employee and worked as a foreman for the C.E. Beckman Company. This ship chandlery and sail making company had roots on the New Bedford waterfront at least as far back as the 1850s and is still in business there today. Durant suggested that Cap have the mainsail cut down to a Marconi or triangular "leg o' mutton" sail, thus eliminating the deteriorated section. Cap did as Durant advised. It was a decision motivated by reality and another sign of the times.

Admiral of the Seuss Navy

The first children's book that Theodor Seuss Geisel wrote and illustrated was published in 1937. The book was *And To Think That I Saw It On Mulberry Street*, and the author, who was born in Springfield, would come to be better known by millions of children and parents as Dr. Seuss. The author no doubt celebrated the book's publication, especially as it had been rejected twenty-seven times before one publisher, Vanguard Press, finally said yes.

Captain Tucker's honorary certificate, created by Dr. Seuss, from the Esso Oil Company. *Collection of Donald F. Tucker.*

At about that time, Dr. Seuss also worked to create advertising campaigns for Standard Oil, a part of which was Esso (later Exxon and ExxonMobil). In this capacity, he illustrated two humorous booklets of information for recreational power boaters, published by the "Makers and Marketers of Essomarine Oils and Greases." Because Esso had a marine division that specialized in lubricants for marine applications, and Captain Tucker was a garage owner and Esso dealer, Cap received booklets titled "Secrets of the Deep, or the Perfect Yachtsman" (1935) and "Secrets of the Deep, Volume II, Aquatints by Dr. Seuss" (1936).

One day, a visitor who was on his way to Cape Cod stopped at Captain Tucker's garage in Fairhaven. The visitor was none other than Dr. Seuss himself, and he was there to deliver a certificate proclaiming Cap to be an "Admiral of the Seuss Navy." There was little ceremony involved, and it is likely that Dr. Seuss simply handed the certificate to whoever was there at the time, chatted a bit and went on his way. Still, it was a keepsake that displayed the unmistakable writing and illustrative style that multitudes of readers have come to enjoy.

Ice

During the 1930s, ice became less and less of a cargo for schooners. Still, Captain Tucker did obtain an occasional charter to carry ice. The Old Colony Railroad freighted this cold cargo to the end of the line in Fairhaven at Hathaway-Braley Wharf, where workers slid the 200- to 250-pound blocks down planks from the rail cars directly onto the schooner. Once loaded, wood shavings were placed between the blocks, and the top was covered with canvas to keep the cargo from melting during delivery to Cuttyhunk, the Vineyard, Nantucket, Block Island and Fishers Island.

Oysters

During the 1930s, Captain Tucker continued to freight an occasional load of oysters. But like the *Coral*, the Rhode Island oyster industry was wiped out by the hurricane of 1938.

"The great hurricane of 1938 silted beds and put an end to about 80 percent of them, inflicting incalculable loss on vessels, shore property, and equipment," wrote John M. Kochiss in *Oystering from New York to Boston*. "Within hours the industry was practically obliterated."

Bill Talbot, who owned oyster beds, put it in more personal terms:

> *The Higgins Oyster Company had a foreman called Peterson. In the last of July, he come over and said, "Billy, you've got $35,000 worth of oysters on your beds." I had a hundred acres.*
>
> *And he said, "Leave it there because there's going to be less oysters next year. You'll get another 50 cents a bushel."*
>
> *Well, after the hurricane, I never even had an oyster shop or an oyster boat or an oyster bed.*

CHAPTER 11

After the Storm

B ill Tucker had to get off the *Coral* fast.

Over and over, the hurricane wind and waves drove the *Coral* sideways back and forth against the rocks on Goat Island. Only a short interval between the waves let the schooner retreat enough to let him regain his balance before the next wave hit. In all the commotion, Bill caught a glimpse of some men standing on the shore, probably men from the torpedo station responding to the distressed vessel. This was his chance to get off the *Coral*.

He tied one end of a line to a life ring and the other end to the schooner. He quickly threw the life ring into the water toward the men. Before long the wind had floated the life ring ashore, where the responders secured the line to a tree. Bill latched onto the line and pulled himself ashore, hand over hand.

By now it was late in the day. With the phone lines down and all electricity lost, there was no way that he could get in touch with his family in Fairhaven. Bill could do nothing more than leave the *Coral* where she was and try to return home. In a stroke of luck, he met up with and got a ride from a man from Fairhaven who worked at the torpedo station, Al Plante. In all, six passengers set out for Fairhaven, dodging water and fallen trees on the roadway, until they reached a point where the wreckage before them halted their trek. Bill then recalled that a cousin of his father's, Minot Tucker, lived somewhere nearby. The travelers eventually found the house. They were welcomed in and thankfully found a place to sleep on Minot's parlor floor, although Bill no doubt relived the day's events over and over again in his mind. The next morning, they set out again.

When Bill finally reached home, he learned that Captain Tucker had tried to reach the *Coral* on the day of the hurricane. His father lived by the barometer, and when he saw how it was dropping, he immediately set out for Newport. By the time he reached the Old Stone Bridge in Tiverton, though, he could go no farther. The authorities had closed the bridge because of the rising water. It was mid-afternoon. Conditions worsened by the minute, so it made no sense to even think of trying to go the long way around and cross at Bristol.

As the water level at the bridge continued to rise, Cap helped two women who couldn't start their car to get on their way. Dark eventually closed in, and Cap found a place in Tiverton where he could sleep in his car for the night. At home, having no information, Mrs. Tucker was a nervous wreck, worrying about both her husband and son.

By the next morning, the weather had cleared, the tide had gone down and the bridge was passable, so Cap continued his journey. Unbeknownst to either Bill or Captain Tucker, it is likely that father and son passed each other on the way. When he finally reached Newport, a Captain Johnson at the torpedo station informed him that he had to get the *Coral* out of there. To speed things along, the officer sent a truckload of line, blocks-and-tackles and other gear. The first thing Cap did then was drag to find the anchor that was lost during the storm. He then canvassed and battened any openings in the schooner. Because the *Coral* was at the shoreline, he next tunneled an anchor chain from one side of the *Coral* to the other through the sand underneath. Finally, he connected both ends of the chain together with a turnbuckle, right between the foremast and the mainmast. The chain was used in pulling the boat free.

After the *Coral* was pumped out and floating, she was towed to Peirce & Kilburn shipyard in Fairhaven by Tom Tilton aboard Freddie Wilbur's *Quest* out of Menemsha.

EVER OPTIMISTIC, AND PERHAPS A BIT DESPERATE

The extent of the damage to the *Coral* became apparent as, inch by inch, the marine railway at Peirce & Kilburn hauled the schooner out of the water. It was a heartbreaking sight, especially as the hurricane had already sent ten feet of water through the garage, ruining the boiler and all tools and equipment. That alone wiped out the source of 80 percent

Workers repair the *Coral* at Peirce and Kilburn shipyard, Fairhaven, following the hurricane of 1938. *Photograph by Albert Cook Church; Collection of Donald F. Tucker.*

of the family's income. Ever optimistic, and perhaps a bit desperate, Cap decided to have the *Coral* repaired. The workers at Peirce and Kilburn spent many weeks trying to rejuvenate the vessel, but the actual cost outdistanced Cap's projected costs. The repair work had to cease, but the *Coral* could now at least float on her own. She was towed to a spot that Mr. Taylor, as he was always referred to, provided on the north side of his marine construction company's yard.

Needless to say, in addition to the difficulties of the Great Depression, the hurricane brought on an additional strain, as it did for many people, both financially and emotionally. Thankfully, all family members survived.

CAPTAIN TUCKER, THE YACHTSMAN

The hurricane of 1938 wiped out both sources of income by which Captain Tucker earned the money to support himself and his family. It was only natural for him, then, to look to the coastal waters for work, and it wasn't long before he found a job on a fishing vessel out of Plymouth. This vessel was the *Alice*, a small, two-man dragger that fished for groundfish in Cape Cod Bay.

Working aboard the *Alice* brought in some much-needed income, but Cap didn't find commercial fishing to be greatly to his liking. So for the 1939 warm weather season, Cap served as skipper aboard a handsome little yawl named the *Mistral* out of a village in South Dartmouth known as Padanaram.

Cap's son Bill later recalled two stories his father used to tell about his time on the *Mistral*. In the first, Cap takes a stand in his bid to convince the owner of the yacht to provide him with suitable yachting attire:

The owner of the *Mistral* was a man from Worcester named Smith. It seems that when Smith hired Cap, he told Cap to go and buy himself some uniforms at M.C. Swift's, a store up on Union Street in New Bedford that sold high-quality clothing. Only one thing—don't buy a hat.

"No hat?" Cap asked.

"No. Every year I buy a hat, I never, ever see it on the skipper's head," Smith replied. "No hat."

So, Cap went to M.C. Swift's and did as he was directed. He then went to see Bernie, the boss painter at Kelley's boatyard in Fairhaven.

"Bernie, I want a paint hat, but I want the oldest one you've got."

"What do you want that for?" Bernie asked incredulously. "Here's a new one."

"I don't want a brand new one."

"Well, here, take mine."

"It isn't dirty enough, Bernie. When it gets dirtier, you save it for me."

Eventually, Bernie got Cap a paint hat that was grubby enough to meet his specifications. Then whenever Smith came aboard, Cap on cue donned the old paint hat.

After this occurred a few times, the yacht's owner Smith wised up and demanded, "Let me see that hat a minute."

"What do you want with my hat?"

"I just want to see it a minute," said Smith, who promptly threw it over the side. "Go up tomorrow and get yourself a hat."

This time, as Cap walked up Union Street, he laughed to himself at how he had gotten a kick out of the whole thing.

In another story Bill Tucker remembered, Cap again good naturedly makes his point and the owner amicably agrees. At the end of the sailing season, Smith said, "Boy, you fed good this year."

"Yup, I guess I did," Cap replied.

"You don't believe me?" Smith shot back. "You ought to see the grub bill for this yacht this summer."

"I never saw you refuse any of it."

Smith looked at him and said, "Damn it, you're right, and it was good, too!"

Little did the owner know, but when serving pork chops to Smith and his guests, Cap would cut the tenderloin out of the chops and have them for himself.

THE TOWN OF MATTAPOISETT, just east of Fairhaven, did not escape the ravages of the hurricane of 1938. When the storm subsided, only one vessel in Mattapoisett Harbor remained afloat, the large power yacht, *Kalmia*. In 1941, Captain Tucker worked as skipper aboard this same vessel.

Kalmia was designed by Cox & Stevens of New York City and built in 1909. At a length overall of eighty-three feet, it drew about four feet of water. In 1938, *Kalmia* was owned by a prominent figure in New Bedford, John Duff Jr. of David Duff and Son, a major coal and oil company in the city. *Kalmia* had once been owned by another important New Bedford businessman, John B. Rhodes of J.C. Rhodes & Company, a manufacturer of eyelets. Rhodes passed away aboard the vessel in Oak Bluffs, Martha's Vineyard, in 1935.

The day before the hurricane, *Kalmia* lay at anchor in Mattapoisett Harbor. Aboard were crew members Fred Boehler, Arthur "Husky" Frates and a third man, "Tacky." Whoever made the entries into the *Kalmia* log noted that the weather was cloudy and rainy. The wind came in from the southeast, then from the southwest, and back and forth throughout the day to produce a "heavy sea." The reading on the barometer slowly dropped to 29.75. (A normal reading is 29.92.)

The weather continued its stormy preview the next morning: "Cloudy and blowing in the morning barometer dropping very fast and wind increasing all the time we started to drag anchor went across to Mollys Cove sea very rough and wind S.E. and strong drag anchor and lost same put down the big anchor not much better."

The crew then tried to go offshore, but on reaching the red nun buoy on the way out, they thought better of it and headed back. They managed to tie up at the wharf, but the lines soon parted as the sea and the wind grew stronger. *Kalmia* hastened back to Molly's Cove to ride it out.

By then it was afternoon. By 3:30 p.m., the barometer had dropped to 28.80. By 4:00 p.m., the wind was at hurricane force and increasing. What the writer of the log called a "tidal wave" hit about thirty minutes later.

Kalmia, skippered by Captain Tucker in 1941. The large power yacht was owned by John Duff Jr. of the David Duff and Son Coal and Oil Company, New Bedford. *Collection of Donald F. Tucker.*

Though the crew had set all anchors out, the wind continued to push *Kalmia* backward. For what seemed like hours, Boehler ran the engines at clutch speed, using the same tactic as Bill Tucker in Newport Harbor.

By 11:00 p.m., conditions had calmed enough for a couple of the crew members to go ashore. The worst was over. A little more than a month later the crew traveled aboard *Kalmia* to Florida where they began a six-month stay as reward for their efforts, courtesy of a Duff family member.

The son of crew member Arthur Frates recently remembered the scene in Mattapoisett Harbor the morning after the hurricane. The eight-year-old Bob Frates asked his father if he had been scared. His dad replied, "Not until we turned on the search light and saw roof tops with a chimney on it. We did not know if we were over land or the roof was floating out to sea."

CHAPTER 12

Working for Mr. Taylor

THE *MORGAN* GOES TO MYSTIC

In the spring of 1941, Captain Tucker began working for Taylor Marine Construction, located on Middle Street in Fairhaven. It was one of those temporary jobs that turn into long-term employment. Mr. Taylor needed a consultant to help him move the whaleship *Charles W. Morgan* from South Dartmouth to Mystic, Connecticut. The Marine Historical Association there had purchased the *Morgan* with the intention of making her the centerpiece of a new outdoor museum. Cap was just the person Mr. Taylor needed, someone who had extensive knowledge and experience working aboard a large, wooden sailing vessel.

Captain Tucker first had to bring the *Morgan* to Fairhaven and ready her so that the old whaleship would be seaworthy enough to make the trip. He could not simply tow the *Morgan* to Fairhaven, however. The venerable whaleship required removal from her current home, partially submerged in the sand and surrounded by a cofferdam at the shoreline at Round Hill, the South Dartmouth estate of a well-known figure in the area, Colonel Green.

Colonel Edward H.R. Green was the son of Hetty Green, at one time the richest woman in America. She passed away in 1916 and left an estate of more than $100 million. In 1924, the colonel purchased the *Morgan* to preserve her as a prominent artifact and symbol of the New Bedford whaling era and to foster continued interest among the public. He funded *Whaling Enshrined*, an organization that restored and

The *Charles W. Morgan* at Round Hill, South Dartmouth, after the hurricane. 1938. *Collection of Donald F. Tucker.*

established a marine park at Round Hill where the *Morgan* would remain until her removal to Mystic.

In time, the whaleship was retrieved and brought to Union Wharf in Fairhaven. On November 5, 1941, the *Morgan* departed Union Wharf with Captain Tucker, the only professional mariner aboard, and a crew of eleven. William H. Tripp, curator of the New Bedford Whaling Museum, served as master of the ship. Historian and newspaperman Everett S. Allen signed on as "boatsteerer" and recorded his own observations and sentiments. Taylor provided the rest of the crew.

According to the plan, the Coast Guard cutter *General Greene* would tow the *Morgan* up the Mystic River to Mystic Seaport. Captain Tucker strongly disagreed, arguing that the *Morgan* would not be able to make her way through the narrow open bridges while on a stern tow (towed by a line from the stern of the vessel in front of her).

When they arrived off the Mystic River, the skipper of the *General Greene* could be seen peering up the river with his binoculars. He realized that a stern tow would not provide enough control over the *Morgan* to guide her through the bridges. An alongside tow, in which the cutter was to push the *Morgan* from the side and aft, was ruled out because there would not be enough room to make it through the bridges. A decision was made to tie up at the Coast Guard Academy at New London until someone figured out how to get the *Morgan* the rest of the way.

Raymond Covill was a young teen in 1941 when he rowed in a skiff he kept at Hathaway-Braley Wharf over to Union Wharf in Fairhaven, where he photographed the *Charles W. Morgan. Courtesy of Raymond Covill.*

At New London, Taylor's crew packed their bags and were ready to head home. But when Taylor's superintendent showed up to pick up the crew, he told Cap that Mr. Taylor wanted him to stay aboard until they reached Mystic. Captain Tucker agreed, and the super assured him that a crew would arrive to help him finish the journey. The crew turned out to be a group of Sea Scouts who gave Captain Tucker a fit by not keeping out of the rigging.

On November 8, a tugboat that was much smaller than the *General Greene* made the final leg with the *Morgan.* Even though we say the tugboat "towed" the *Morgan,* it actually snugged up against the *Morgan's* port quarter and pushed the whaling vessel. They made it through the drawbridge by mere inches.

The chronicles of maritime history contain many well-known stories of sailing vessels on the high seas that rescued shipwrecked or marooned sailors. One such rescue has gone largely unnoticed, however. True, it didn't exactly take place on the high seas, but it did involve the *Morgan* on her 1941 voyage from Fairhaven to Mystic.

As the whaleship neared Mystic, the crew heard someone shouting for help from the cold November waters. It was a young man, and the crew threw him a line and hauled him up. The crew didn't know this but, in reality, the fellow just wanted a ride on the old whaler. He had jumped out of a sailboat that he and his buddy had been in nearby.

When he landed on deck, they asked Cap what they should do with him.

"Lock him in the brig 'til we can get him ashore to the police," came Cap's order.

There was no brig aboard the *Morgan*, but the young man did not know that. He jumped back on the rail and dove back into the river, where his buddy in the sailboat picked him up.

Captain Tucker, who was a great josher, thought that that was one of his best.

CARETAKER OF THE *MORGAN*

When the *Morgan* had been safely delivered, the crew and the visitors all went home except for Captain Tucker. He stayed on as the *Morgan*'s caretaker, taking a room in a boardinghouse in Mystic.

For about a month all seemed to go well, but for the fact that Cap and the family would be living apart for who knows how long. Then, life took on an added seriousness for the Tuckers as well as the rest of the nation with the attack on Pearl Harbor on December 7.

December was particularly difficult for the family. Captain Tucker was away at Mystic, and son Frank had been aboard the USS *San Francisco* in Pearl Harbor on the "date that will live in infamy." The family agonized for days until they finally received word that Frank had survived. The euphoria did not last long, however. Less than a year later, Francis J. Tucker was killed in the Great Naval Battle of Guadalcanal on November 13, 1942.

Despite this tragedy for the family, life went on. As caretaker, Cap kept the pumps of the *Morgan* going, and he later helped Taylor's crew put on a new deck. Providing a measure of relief, Captain Tucker's son Bill drove the family down to Mystic on Sundays in his pride and joy, a 1938 Buick four-door Century model automobile.

Cap's work aboard the *Morgan* lasted through the spring of 1942. With the demands of the war effort, the navy needed dock builders, and Taylor was hired for some of that work. Because Cap had a good reputation with Taylor and Taylor's crews, he was asked to stay on with the company. Cap traveled from Fairhaven to Newport by carpool every day for the rest of World War II, working ten to twelve hours a day.

Zeb "Acquires" the Coral

Zeb Tilton had always admired the *Coral*. At some point during Zeb's financial difficulties in the late 1930s and early '40s, he made an arrangement with Captain Tucker to bring the *Coral* to the Vineyard and rebuild her. Zeb hoped to ultimately put the schooner back to work. The task would be formidable, however, for the *Coral* was in pretty rough shape. The engine

The *Coral* in Fairhaven. Captain Tucker (left) and sons Claude Jr. (center) and Donald. Both the bow and the stern of the *Coral* have already "hogged down," indicating stress caused by resting on the bottom during low tide. 1940. *Photograph by Helen Tucker Davidson; Collection of Donald F. Tucker.*

no longer operated. The mainmast had no boom. The bow and the stern showed signs of "hogging down," due to the center of the hull resting on the shallow harbor bottom north of Taylor's wharf. Nevertheless, the two men had known each other for years, and Cap believed that Zeb would get the job done.

In 1944, Cap hauled out the sails that he had stored in his cellar and readied the yawl boat, which lay under canvas in his yard at 84 Main Street. Then he loaded them aboard the schooner. A workboat then towed the *Coral* to the Vineyard, where Zeb succeeded in replacing the bowsprit, which had remained attached to the hull despite signs of rot. The work proceeded slowly, though. His wife Grace's extended illness and his own medical bills from an eye operation finally brought Zeb's attempt to revitalize the *Coral* to an end.

The story goes that Zeb had agreed to pay Cap for the *Coral* when he brought her to the Vineyard, but no payment was ever received. This did not bother Cap in any way, though, because he knew Zeb had every intention of paying. In the end, a tug simply towed the *Coral* from Vineyard Haven back to her home in Fairhaven. It would be the *Coral*'s final journey.

When the *Coral* returned to Fairhaven, Mr. Taylor allowed Cap to berth her on the north side of Taylor property at an unused decrepit dock. There the *Coral* stayed, bow facing inward as if acknowledging that she would never sail again.

THE LUCY EVELYN

Captain Tucker, working for Taylor, sailed aboard the three-masted schooner *Lucy Evelyn* as she was towed to Chelsea Creek, near Boston, for major repairs. The *Lucy Evelyn* was built in Harrington, Maine, in 1916. After her sailing years, many people knew her as a tourist attraction on a New Jersey beach. As a coaster, she was a familiar sight from Nova Scotia to the southern states to the Caribbean, often bringing lumber from Maine to New York and returning with coal. In later years, the coaster carried many loads of granite.

While in New Bedford at the Pocahontas Coal Company north of the bridge, the *Lucy Evelyn* was damaged when a storm blew up northeast. The schooner was not secured properly, and her bowsprit became tangled in the coal-handling derrick there, twisting the *Lucy Evelyn* so that she opened up badly.

The *Lucy Evelyn* was moved to the New Bedford Gas and Edison Light Company dock where Taylor looked after her. Captain Tucker and another Taylor man worked twelve hours on, twelve hours off, seven days a week, running the pumps and making sure she stayed afloat. Donald Tucker has fond memories of going with his brother Claude to keep their father company. The captain would sit around the comfortably heated cabin and read by the hour, since there wasn't much to do except to take soundings and run the gasoline pumps, if needed.

When it came time to tow the *Lucy Evelyn* to Chelsea Creek for repairs, Taylor asked Captain Tucker who he could get to go with him. Cap insisted on Ben Waterworth. An old oyster boat came down from Boston to New Bedford to do the towing. The towboat and the *Lucy Evelyn* got as far as the east end of the Cape Cod Canal when a pretty good wind came out of the north. If they continued at that point, they would have had to head right into that wind as they made their way across Cape Cod and Massachusetts Bays. The towboat didn't have a lot of power, so her skipper decided to wait there at Sandwich.

After two days, the wind shifted southwest, and Captain Tucker got after the skipper to get going. Out in the bay, the towboat skipper asked Captain Tucker to put some sail up on the *Lucy Evelyn* to give him an assist. Cap and Waterworth got the main sail and fore sail on her, and the *Lucy Evelyn* began to almost outrun the boat towing her. The towboat had to speed up just to keep the tow line out of the water.

Approaching Boston, they took the sails down but found that sailing her had opened up some seams. The *Lucy Evelyn* began leaking badly, and by the time they got into Chelsea Creek, the pumps were running constantly. After a while, Captain Tucker and Waterworth found some old mattresses, and using long poles, they stuffed the ticking from the mattresses down into the areas where she was leaking the worst. This managed to stem the flow considerably.

Because they had waited at Sandwich, the *Lucy Evelyn* was late and lost her turn on the marine railway at Chelsea. The schooner remained there, with Captain Tucker and Waterworth aboard, for two months until she was hauled. When Waterworth had accepted the job, he had been concerned that he would not get two weeks' work out of it.

With the *Lucy Evelyn* again shipshape, she was bound for New Bedford. Captain Zeb Tilton, at an advanced age, and others sailed her back. The *Lucy Evelyn* had no engine, however, and did not have the services of a tug.

This prevented her from going through the Cape Cod Canal, but she did make it around Cape Cod safely.

The *Lucy Evelyn* last worked under sail as a Cape Verde packet. The coaster ended her career in Beach Haven, New Jersey, as a tourist attraction from 1948 until her destruction by fire in 1972.

The Vindex

Following the war, Taylor Marine Construction remained busy with dock building and salvage work. It used its small tugboat named the *Vindex* to tow workboats such as barges, scows and lighters. Coincidentally, Captain Byron Hallock, who had served as captain aboard the *Coral*, later worked aboard an iron-hulled, sloop yacht also named *Vindex*.

A workboat such as one used by Taylor could get very heavy, as it might be loaded with dock pilings, creosote timbers or a variety of tools needed at a worksite. The *Vindex* was equipped with twin gasoline engines, one built in 1917 and the other in 1918. With engines over thirty years old and the workboats they towed so heavy, the *Vindex* could be underpowered in some conditions and have a difficult time reaching the job with any speed.

In time, the man who operated the *Vindex* retired,

Captain Tucker working for the Frank C. Taylor Company, a marine construction firm in Fairhaven. Early 1940s. *Collection of Donald F. Tucker.*

and Cap took over. Knowing the limitations of the *Vindex*, whenever Cap had to go through a congested area such as Woods Hole or Quicks Hole, he wasn't above asking Mr. Taylor to hire the *Anton Dohrn*, a small workboat, to give him an assist.

Cap continued to work for Mr. Taylor until the 1960s, when he retired after a long, productive and interesting career.

Previous page, top: Workers aboard the Taylor Marine Construction Company tug *Vindex* prepare to raise and remove the sunken tug *Plymouth*, January 27, 1938. The *Plymouth* collided with the collier *Everett* at the east end of the Cape Cod Canal. Note the worker operating the air pump for the hardhat divers in the middle of the *Vindex*. Captain Tucker would eventually skipper the *Vindex* for many years. *Courtesy of the U.S. Army Corps of Engineers.*

Previous page, bottom: The *Vindex*, not seen in the photograph, tows a lighter to a job at Martha's Vineyard. The tug *Anton Dohrn*, on the left, helps out with a side tow "on the hip." *Collection of Donald F. Tucker.*

CHAPTER 13

Later Years

After World War II, new owners George and Herman Schwartz expanded the old Park Garage and transformed it into Park Motors, with the familiar neon Oldsmobile sign. This meant that Captain Tucker and his family had to move. They found a small cottage at 97 Middle Street,

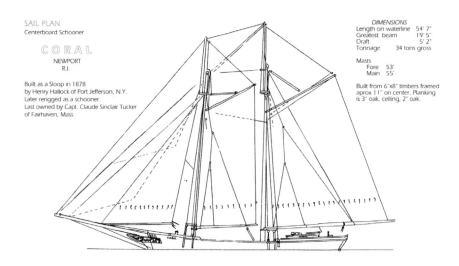

SAIL PLAN
Centerboard Schooner

CORAL
NEWPORT
R.I.

Built as a Sloop in 1878
by Henry Hallock of Port Jefferson, N.Y.
Later rerigged as a schooner.
Last owned by Capt. Claude Sinclair Tucker
of Fairhaven, Mass

DIMENSIONS
Length on waterline   54' 7"
Greatest beam   19' 5"
Draft   5' 2"
Tonnage   34 tons gross

Masts
Fore   53'
Main   55'

Built from 6"x8" timbers framed
aprox 11" on center. Planking
is 3" oak, ceiling, 2" oak.

Sail plan of the *Coral*, drawn up with Captain Tucker's permission by a potential buyer in the 1950s. The information and dimensions were added to the original drawing at a later date. *Collection of Donald F. Tucker*

The *Coral* at Taylor's. Circa 1950. *Courtesy of Captains Doug and Linda Lee.*

not far from the southeast corner of Middle and Bridge Streets, where they established a large garden just to the south. One day during high school biology class, Donald Tucker was startled to see half of the house he was born in traveling down Huttleston Avenue, on its way to a new location on Hope Avenue.

129

In the 1950s, a prospective buyer from Washington, D.C., looked at the *Coral* and saw some potential for rebirth. He went so far as to study the vessel's appearance to draw up a sail plan, but in the end nothing ever came of it. Time, tide, weather and vandals continued to take their toll on the schooner.

Hurricane Carol brought more devastation to Fairhaven in 1954. At Taylor's dock, the storm disassembled the *Coral* once and for all. The storm flood also destroyed the collection of photos, documents, logs and journals relating to the *Coral* that the Tucker family kept at their home at 97 Middle Street. In the wake of the hurricane, Captain and Mrs. Tucker decided to move inland where the surging waters of the harbor would not reach them in the future.

The family had established roots in town more than thirty years before, however, and so they chose 116 Washington Street for their new home. It was less than a mile away from both their old home and the *Coral's* final resting place at the waterfront.

Retirement brought Captain and Mrs. Tucker some of their happiest times together. They spent their days making home improvements, tending a

The end of a fine vessel. The *Coral* in Fairhaven. 1960. *Collection of Donald F. Tucker.*

Captain and Mrs. Tucker on their fiftieth wedding anniversary. 1967. *Collection of Donald F. Tucker.*

big garden and canning vegetables late into the fall each year. In 1967, they celebrated their fiftieth wedding anniversary. All five surviving children settled nearby, keeping the folks busy with grandchildren—all nineteen of them. Grandson Tom, Donald's son, continues to work in the maritime trade.

In later years, historians and authors John Leavitt and Captain Francis "Biff" Bowker of Mystic Seaport interviewed Cap about his days operating a small, family-owned coasting schooner. Cap was also happy to pass down what he knew to a young couple who owned the schooner *L.A. Jeffrey*. The couple often joined Cap and Mrs. Tucker at the house for a Saturday night meal and hours of schooner stories. Fortunately, son Donald Tucker also recorded several hours of interviews with his father.

Epilogue

C aptain Tucker and the coasting schooner *Coral* were among the last of their kind. With their passing, a way of life that existed for more than two centuries came a bit closer to extinction.

The *Coral* sailed for sixty years, the last twenty-three with Captain Tucker as owner and operator. One can't help but think that the work of Captain Henry Hallock in building and rebuilding the *Coral*, as well as the attention paid to her well being by subsequent owners, captains and crews, including Captain Tucker, all contributed to her long life. In the end, it took the devastation caused by both the great hurricane of 1938 and the Great Depression to bring about the demise of the little *Coral*. Her longevity stands as a tribute to her guardians throughout the years.

Under Captain Tucker, a combination of factors enabled the *Coral* to continue hauling cargo and bring in an income during those last decades. Cap believed that care and maintenance of the schooner was essential, and he settled in a town where the repair facilities and qualified yard crews were close at hand. In Fairhaven, Cap was with "his people."

Captain Tucker was also wise to take advantage of niche markets when they became available, such as delivering cordwood that was more "user friendly" from Mattapoisett to Newport and delivering gasoline from New Bedford to Nantucket. Cap also had the security of owning and operating the Park Garage and did not need to rely on the schooner as the sole source of the family income. It also didn't hurt that the Tucker boys looked forward to sailing and working with their dad aboard the schooner, which helped keep down costs.

Captain Tucker at the helm of the *Coral*. Mid-1920s.
Collection of Donald F. Tucker.

In the 1960s, a subsequent owner of the Taylor site decided to increase the size of the construction yard. To do this, he built a cofferdam around the north side of the property, and then backfilled it with stone and gravel. The area included the spot where Captain Tucker's schooner was gradually going to pieces. The *Coral* lies buried there today, about fifty feet west of Middle Street, and across the water and to the south of the public boat ramp parking lot. The site is now part of the Linberg Marine yard. Some relics have survived, however, including Cap's binoculars and the *Coral*'s life ring, running lights and compass. Part of the *Coral*'s trailboards hangs on the wall of the Black Dog Tavern, owned by Captain Robert Douglas, on Martha's Vineyard.

The Fairhaven waterfront of today retains its maritime character, where the focus is on repair and maintenance of fishing vessels, recreational and large luxury craft, whale watch boats and historic wooden vessels. Fairhaven is also the final resting place of many mariners and members of their families, including Captain and Mrs. Tucker. Mrs. Tucker passed away in 1968 at age seventy-five. Cap joined her in 1980 at age eighty-eight. The headstone they share in Riverside Cemetery is engraved with a likeness of the *Coral*, a fitting remembrance to the schooner and their lives together.

The era of the freight-carrying cargo schooner has passed, but it gave rise to a new era: the vacation windjammer trade. As one captain in the Maine windjammer fleet observed, "This is commercial sail, still. We're still hauling

The *Coral*'s running lights. *Photograph by Robert Demanche.*

A view from the schooner *Grace Bailey* of vacationers aboard the *Stephen Taber*. July 1996. *Photograph by Robert Demanche.*

Awaiting the start of the annual Great Schooner Race off the coast of Maine. July 1996. *Photograph by Robert Demanche.*

cargo. Our cargo walks on board instead of being carried on board." The vessels in this trade include original schooners that have been rebuilt and schooners that were newly constructed for this purpose.

A cruise on today's windjammer calls to mind a place and time when life's tempo was more of a walk and less of a mad rush. It offers the passenger a chance to glory in the beauty of our coastal waters, experience a taste of the days of working sail or simply lie back aboard a schooner and bask in the ambiance of the day.

The era of the coasting schooner captain also has passed, giving rise to a new type of captain in the windjammer trade. Beyond experiencing the joys and responsibilities of owning and sailing a large wooden vessel, the job might require this captain at times to be part tour guide, part hotelier, part entertainment director or part educator.

Though it may not make sense to some people, the captains of today's windjammers might not make riches, but neither would they trade places with anyone else in the world. If Captain Tucker were here today, he would think of the *Coral*, smile and understand.

Bibliography

Allen, Everett S. "Development of a Seaport." *A Picture History of Fairhaven.* Edited by Joseph D. Thomas and Marsha McCabe. New Bedford, MA: Spinner Publications, 1986.

Beers & Co., J.H. "Representative Men and Old Families of Southeastern Massachusetts." *Rhodes Family Geneology Pages; Rhodes Family of Taunton and New Bedford, MA.* http://rhodesfamily.org/rhodes_family_of_taunton_ma.php (accessed February 5, 2013).

Bunting, W.H. *Portrait of a Port: Boston, 1852–1914.* First paperback. Cambridge, MA: Belknap Press of Harvard University Press, 1994.

Burroughs, Polly. *Zeb: A Celebrated Schooner Life.* 1st. Guilford, CT: Globe Pequot Press, 2005.

C.E. Beckman Company, Marine Wholesale & Service Station. http://www.cebeckman.com/ (accessed November 8, 2012).

"Certificates of Enrollment, February 1829-June 1911, Port of New London, Connecticut." Microfilm records available at the New Bedford [MA] Free Public Library archives.

Chapelle, Howard I. *The History of American Sailing Ships.* Reprint. New York, NY: Bonanza Books, 1935.

Christian Science Monitor.

CNIC/Naval Station Newport. *History.* www.cnic.navy.mil/Newport/About/History/index.htm (accessed December 5, 2012).

"Cook Borden and Company Account Books (MS 288)." *Special Collections and University Archives, University Libraries, UMass Amherst.* http://library.umass.edu/spcoll/ead/mums288.pdf (accessed February 2, 2013).

Dr. Seuss National Memorial Sculpture Garden at the Springfield Museums. http://www.catinthehat.org/ (accessed December 26, 2012).

Fairhaven Shipyard Companies, Inc. http://fairhavenshipyard.com/ (accessed February 18, 2013).

Fairhaven Star.

Fowler, William. "New England Coastal Schooners." Unpublished videorecording of talk presented at the Old Dartmouth Historical Society/New Bedford [MA] Whaling Museum, 1995.

Gale, George. "Log of the 'Coral.'" Unpublished manuscripts available at the Old Dartmouth Historical Society/New Bedford [MA] Whaling Museum, 1923–5.

Goddard, Thomas P.I., Caroline Hazard Goddard, Douglas K. Lee, and Linda J. Lee. *Fly Rails and Flying Jibs: Coasting Schooner Photographs by Robert H.I. Goddard.* Mystic, CT: Mystic Seaport, 2011.

Grayson, Stan. *American Marine Engines, 1885-1950.* Marblehead, MA: Devereux Books, 2008.

Hallock, Byron Whitfield. *Forty Years Windjammer.* Edited by Albert G. Hallock. Floral Park, NY: Jeffrey Hallock, 1995.

The Historical Society of Greater Port Jefferson. *Tour II.* www.portjeffhistorical.org (accessed February 8, 2013).

History of Glenwood Stove & Range Company. http://goodtimestove.com/faqs/42-stove-foundries/354-history-of-glenwood-stove-range-company (accessed December 17, 2012).

Inventory of the Whaling Enshrined, Incorporated, Records in the New Bedford Whaling Museum Research Library. http://www.whalingmuseum.org/explore/library/finding-aids/mss45 (accessed March 20, 2013).

Keyes, George. "George Gale." Unpublished videorecording, n.d.

Kochiss, John M. *Oystering from New York to Boston.* 1st. Middletown, CT: Wesleyan University Press, 1974.

Labaree, Benjamin W., Jr., William M. Fowler, Edward W. Sloan, John B. Hattendorf, Jeffrey J. Safford, and Andrew W. German. *America and the Sea: A Maritime History.* Mystic, CT: Mystic Seaport Museum, Inc., 1998.

Leavitt, John F. *Wake of the Coasters.* 2nd ed. Mystic, CT: Mystic Seaport Museum, Incorporated, 1984.

Lewis, Arthur H. *The Day They Shook the Plum Tree.* New York: Harcourt, Brace & World, Inc., 1963.

Martha's Vineyard Museum. www.mvmuseum.org (accessed February 13, 2013).

Martha's Vineyard Times.

Merchant Vessels of the United States, Annual Lists. Treasury Department, Bureau of Navigation.

Mitchell, David. "Glimpse Fairhaven's Nautical Heritage at 80 Middle Street." Fairhaven, MA: Unpublished manuscript, May 2010.

Morgan, Charles S. "New England Coasting Schooners." *The American Neptune,* 1963.

Morris, Paul C. *Schooners and Schooner Barges.* 1st ed. Orleans, MA: Lower Cape Publishing Co., 1984.

Mystic River Bridge Opens—Today in History. connecticuthistory.org/mystic-river-bridge-opens-today-in-history (accessed January 7, 2013).

Nantucket Inquirer and Mirror.

New Bedford Morning Mercury.

New Bedford Standard-Times.

New Bedford Sunday Standard-Times.

New Bedford Sunday Times.

New York Times.

Parker, W.J. Lewis. *The Great Coal Schooners of New England, 1870–1909.* Mystic, CT: Marine Historical Association, Inc., 1948.

Phillips, Arthur Sherman. *The Phillips History of Fall River.* Fall River, MA: Privately printed; Dover Press, 1944–6.

Providence Evening Journal.

Providence Journal.

Quincy Ledger.

"Report of the Sailors' Snug Harbor." Boston, MA: Geo. H. Ellis Co., 1960.

Sea Kindly: Windjammer Wisdom for Everyone. DVD. Directed by Rich Holzer. Produced by Dolphin's Eye. 2009.

"Ship Licenses Issued to Vessels under Twenty Tons and Ship Licenses on Enrollments Issued Out of the Port of Providence, Rhode Island 1793-1939, Vol. II." The Survey of Federal Archives, The National Archives Project, Providence, Rhode Island, 1941.

"Ship Registers and Enrollments of Newport, Rhode Island 1790–1939, Vol. I." The Survey of Federal Archives, The National Archives Project, Rhode Island, 1938–1941.

Snow, Ralph Linwood, and Captain Douglas K. Lee. *A Shipyard in Maine: Percy & Small and the Great Schooners.* Gardiner, ME: Tilbury House, Publishers, 1999.

Stackpole, Matthew. "'Charles W. Morgan:' Arriving in Mystic in November 1941." *Mystic Seaport Magazine* (Fall/Winter 2011): 12–13.

Talbot, Wilfred D., interview by Donald F. Tucker and Robert Demanche.

(October 11, 1996).

Taylor, Kate. "Slow and Steady." *Kate Taylor.* Composition by Zach Weisner and James Taylor. 1977, 1978. Vinyl audio recording.

Taylor, Old Captain. "Secrets of the Deep, or the Perfect Yachtsman." Makers and Marketers of Essomarine Oils and Greases, 1935. First published 1934.

———. "Secrets of the Deep, Volume II, Aquatints by Dr. Seuss." Makers and Marketers of Essomarine Oils and Greases, 1936.

Thorndike, Virginia L. *Windjammer Watching on the Coast of Maine.* 2nd ed. Camden, ME: Down East Books, 1993.

Tucker, Bill, interview by Donald F. Tucker. (July 25, 1997).

Tucker, Captain Claude S., interview by Donald F. Tucker. (1960s–'70s).

Tucker, Captain Claude S., interview by Captain Francis E. "Biff" Bowker. (January 24, 1977).

Tucker, Donald F., interview by Robert Demanche. (2011–2012).

Tucker, Donald F., Robert Demanche, and Caroline B. Tucker. *A Coastal Schooner Life on Southern New England Waters: Captain Claude S. Tucker, the 'Coral,' and the End of an Era.* Fairhaven, MA: Privately published, 1999.

U.S. Enters World War I. http://memory.loc.gov/ammen/today/apr06.html (accessed December 5, 2012).

Vineyard Gazette.

Yachting.

Index

About the Authors

CARRIE TUCKER is married to Captain Claude S. Tucker's seafaring grandson, Tom. In addition to raising the next generation of sailing Tuckers in coastal Mattapoisett, she works as a school librarian in East Bridgewater and reference librarian in Marshfield.

DONALD TUCKER, son of Captain Claude S. Tucker, is a member of the U.S. Coast Guard Auxiliary in Fairhaven and a veteran of the United States Air Force. Don and his wife, Lois, raised their four children in Fairhaven no more than five hundred feet from the harbor.

ROBERT DEMANCHE, the book's primary author, grew up in Fairhaven. A longtime friend of the Tuckers and contributing author to *A Picture History of Fairhaven*, he especially enjoys family holiday gatherings where tales of modern maritime life are told.